A Commentary on Gabriel Marcel's *The Mystery of Being*

A Commentary on Gabriel Marcel's
The Mystery of Being

Thomas C. Anderson
EMERITUS PROFESSOR OF PHILOSOPHY
MARQUETTE UNIVERSITY

MARQUETTE
UNIVERSITY

PRESS

Marquette Studies in Philosophy
No. 46
Andrew Tallon, Series Editor

LIBRARY OF CONGRESS CATALOGING-IN-PUBLICATION DATA

Anderson, Thomas C., 1935-
A commentary on Gabriel Marcel's : the mystery of being / Thomas
C. Anderson.
p. cm. — (Marquette studies in philosophy ; no. 46)
Includes bibliographical references and index.
ISBN-13: 978-0-87462-669-8 (pbk. : alk. paper)
ISBN-10: 0-87462-669-2 (pbk. : alk. paper)
1. Marcel, Gabriel, 1889-1973. Mystère de l'être. 2. Ontology. 3. Faith.
4. Reality. I. Title.
B2430.M253A53 2006
110—dc22
2006031620

Cover photo of Gabriel Marcel taken by his son, Jean-Marie Marcel.

♾The paper used in this publication meets the minimum requirements of the
American National Standard for Information Sciences—
Permanence of Paper for Printed Library Materials, ANSI Z39.48-1992.

MARQUETTE UNIVERSITY PRESS
MILWAUKEE

The Association of Jesuit University Presses

TABLE OF CONTENTS

COMMENTATOR'S PREFACE

Over the past decade, there has been renewed interest in the thought of the twentieth century French philosopher, Gabriel Marcel, sometimes (to his dismay) referred to as a Christian existentialist. Very important philosophical works of his, namely, the two volumes of *The Mystery of Being*, *Creative Fidelity*, and "Concrete Approaches to Investigating the Ontological Mystery," which have been out of print, have been reissued.[1] An English translation of his final work, the autobiographical *Awakenings*, has recently been published[2] as has a translation of one of his most important plays, "The Broken World."[3] Finally, a collection of essays containing his philosophical reflections on music is now available.[4] Of course, this renewed interest is welcomed by those who believe that his investigations into the human condition in general and interpersonal relations in particular, including our relations with God, are innovative and insightful. Marcel was among the first to enunciate the distinction between I-

---

1   *The Mystery of Being* was republished by St. Augustine's Press in 2001; *Creative Fidelity* by Fordham University Press in 2002; "Concrete Approaches to Investigating The Ontological Mystery" was republished in *Gabriel Marcel's Perspectives On The Broken World* by Marquette University Press in 1998.

2   By Marquette University Press in 2002.

3   "The Broken World" published in *Gabriel Marcel's Perspectives On The Broken World* by Marquette University Press, 1998. K. R. Hanley deserves special recognition for her translations of that play and many others: *Ghostly Mysteries: A Mystery of Love & The Posthumous Joke* (Milwaukee: Marquette University Press, 2004), *Two Plays By Gabriel Marcel: The Lantern and The Torch of Peace* plus "From Comic Theater to Musical Creation" *a previously unpublished essay by Gabriel Marcel* (Lanham, MD: University Press of America, 1988), *Dramatic Approaches to Creative Fidelity: A Study In The Theater And Philosophy of Gabriel Marcel 1889-1973* (Lanham, MD: University Press of America, 1987), *Two One Act Plays: Dot the I and The Double Expertise* (Lanham, MD: University Press of America, 1986). These last two plays and *The Lantern* are available on two CD audio dramas. For information contact hanleykr@aol.com.

4   *Music and Philosophy: Gabriel Marcel* trans. S. Maddux and R. Wood (Milwaukee: Marquette University Press, 2005).

thou and I-him or her relations, the difference between having and being, the phenomena of the lived body and sensation, the situated character of human existence, the natures of fidelity, hope, and love and their primacy in human life, the obscure but real experience of an Absolute Thou, to mention just a few areas. On these and other topics, I believe he continues to have much to teach us, provided we are able to understand his words, and that brings me to the purpose of this book. My experience in reading Marcel and in teaching him to both undergraduate and graduate students for over thirty five years has convinced me that his writings are often not easily understood by even his most attentive and sympathetic readers. As Kenneth Gallagher wrote in his ground breaking study, *The Philosophy of Gabriel Marcel*, "Marcel's thought, while original and fascinating, is so extremely elusive that it is a rare reader for whom it does not seem to cry out for interpretation."[5]

By his own admission, Marcel was not a very systematic thinker. Although there is a discernible order and overall direction to each of his works, instead of following a strict logical progression from one idea to the next, his writings sometimes appear to be random digressions on various topics. This is not to suggest that Marcel violated or ignored basic principles of logic, but rather that he often seems to move from one topic to another without fully explaining either or making clear the exact connection between them. His treatments of particular issues are frequently so sketchy and his arguments in support of his positions so briefly presented that they demand further elaboration. Many times the reason for his brevity seems to be that he has already discussed the particular topic or argument more extensively in earlier works—and he almost presupposes that his reader is familiar with those discussions or will consult them if he or she is not. In this commentary, then, I will offer a more complete explanation of many of his ideas and arguments than Marcel himself does in *The Mystery of Being* and I will present in a more explicit and orderly fashion the often unexpressed logical con-nections among his thoughts. What enables me to do this is that I will bring into my remarks on each chapter many of his treatments of the same topics in other works he published, works written both before and after *The Mystery*....

5   *The Philosophy of Gabriel Marcel* (New York: Fordham University Press, 1962), ix.

This commentary is not meant to take the place of a serious reading of *The Mystery of Being* but to offer a reader assistance in understanding what Marcel is saying there and what he means by what he says. It is written for all those who, though attracted to his thought and work, find them difficult to grasp. In other words, my book is written not just for scholars who have studied Marcel but also for educated people who may or may not have read him but who are interested in entering into the philosophical reflections of a major Catholic thinker of the twentieth century. For that reason, while I cite almost all of his other philosophical works, I have decided not to include references to the secondary literature.

I have chosen to comment on *The Mystery of Being* because in my judgment it contains the most orderly, comprehensive and unified presentation by Marcel of his philosophical endeavors. So many of his other works, for example, *Creative Fidelity, Homo Viator,* and *Tragic Wisdom and Beyond,* are collections of speeches and essays presented or written by him at various times on diverse topics. Others, such as *Metaphysical Journal, Being and Having,* and *Presence and Immortality* are diary like journals containing his early philosophical reflections on many different topics. As a result, those works do not have, nor were they intended to have, the overarching unity and inclusiveness that we find in *The Mystery of Being*. Marcel himself says in that work he is attempting to set forth the "general direction" of his thought and to articulate the connections among its various parts *[I, 34]*. Apparently, he considered that attempt to be successful for in *The Existential Background of Human Dignity,* written ten years later, he states that the two volumes of *The Mystery of Being* enabled him "to achieve the approximate synthesis" of his work.[6] Thus, a commentary on *The Mystery...* will inevitably deal with almost all the major components of Marcel's philosophical thought.

A word about my procedure. Needless to say, I cannot comment on every single sentence in his text and so I will concentrate on the central ideas and arguments he presents and attempt to explain them. Sometimes his meaning in a particular passage is quite clear and little commentary is needed; therefore, I will focus my efforts on those places where he states, but hardly explains, his positions or where his words seem to be particularly obscure. As I said earlier, bringing in his discussions of the same topic in his other works (or in later chapters of *The Mystery ...* for that matter) will often be very helpful in understanding his text. I wish

---

6 EBHD, 3.

that Marcel's chapters had been divided into numbered sections and subsections which could serve as easy reference points for a commentary, but they are not. In working through each chapter, then, I will basically follow the page by page order of his exposition, although sometimes it will be more enlightening to group together in one place all of the things he has to say about a given topic in that chapter and elsewhere. In any case, I will continually use italicized numbers in brackets, for example, *[I, 100]*, to refer the reader to the particular page or pages in *The Mystery* ... that I am addressing. Occasionally, Marcel refers to past and present philosophers and other writers. Most often his references are made just in passing and for that reason it seems unnecessary, and even distracting, to spend time discussing those thinkers. Only when he goes into some detail about a particular person's views, will I address them.

The two volumes of the English version of *The Mystery of Being* that have recently been reprinted consist of a series of talks Marcel gave over a two year period at the University of Aberdeen, Scotland, in 1949 (Volume I) and 1950 (Volume II). They are part of the very prestigious Gifford Lecture Series given every year at one or more Scottish universities. Only scholars who are renowned for their work in the philosophy of religion or natural theology are invited to give those lectures and so the fact that Gabriel Marcel was asked indicates that by the late 1940s he had already attained an international reputation. The lectures were first published in English in Great Britain in 1951 by Harvill Press, Ltd., the same year they were published in French by Aubier Press. The English text we have is said to be a translation from the French one. Volume one was translated by the famous British poet, G. S. Fraser, who later also translated Marcel's *Man Against Mass Society*. Volume two was translated by René Hague, who also translated into English many works of Teillard de Chardin and some of Henri de Lubac. In 1960 Regnery Press published the Harvill English translation in the United States and that is the edition St. Augustine's Press has recently reprinted.

It seems clear from reading them that the lectures in Scotland must have been given in English, for Marcel often takes pains to explain the meaning of French words and phrases to his audience. Nevertheless, the fact remains that what we have in print in English is a translation from the French edition and for this reason I have not hesitated to consult the French text, especially when Marcel's English is unclear.

After all, French was his native language and, while he spoke and wrote excellent English, I presume he could express himself even more clearly and precisely in his native tongue. It is worth noting that on occasion the English translation actually contains words, phrases, even whole sentences that do not appear in the French text. It also, less often, omits words that are in the French edition. Since there is no indication that the translators themselves have added or subtracted them, I assume that was done by Marcel himself either in his original English lecture or afterwards. The problem is that at times the additions and subtractions in English rather significantly alter the meaning of what is present in the French copy. In such cases, for the reason I have stated, I will give priority to the French version.

Since these Gifford lectures were given in 1949 and 1950, they come soon after the end of World War II, during the Cold War between the East and West, and just before the outbreak of the Korean War in June, 1950. The late 40s and early 50s were times of increasing tensions between the Western democracies and the Soviet Union along with its eastern European allies and they marked the beginning of the nuclear arms race. In 1949 the Soviet Union blockaded West Berlin and detonated its first atomic bomb. In 1950 NATO was formed to protect the countries of Western Europe and the Americas from the spread of the Soviet Empire. I review all this history because it helps explain Marcel's frequent pessimistic remarks in these lectures about the state of the world in his day.

I cannot end this preface without acknowledging those who have significantly contributed to my knowledge of Marcel. Special thanks go to all my friends in the Gabriel Marcel Society for their constant stimulation, particularly Thomas Busch, the late Robert Lechner, James Marsh, Thomas Michaud, Astrid and Robert O'Brien, and Teresa Reed. I especially want to acknowledge the assistance of Katherine Rose Hanley who with meticulous care read my entire manuscript. I also owe a great debt to my students who for over thirty five years forced me to clarify and deepen my understanding of Marcel's thought; without them my knowledge of him would be much more superficial. Finally, I will never be able to adequately express my appreciation to my wife, Kay, for her invaluable editorial assistance but most especially for her courage and love during very difficult times.

LIST OF ABBREVIATIONS
FOR FREQUENTLY CITED WORKS OF GABRIEL MARCEL

BH *Being and Having*, trans. K. Farrer (New York: Harper, 1965).

CA "Concrete Approaches to Investigating The Ontological Mystery," in *Gabriel Marcel's Perspectives On The Broken World*, trans K. R. Hanley (Milwaukee: Marquette University Press, 1998).

CF *Creative Fidelity*, trans. R. Rosthal (New York: Fordham University Press, 2002).

EBHD *The Existential Background of Human Dignity* (Cambridge: Harvard University Press, 1971).

HV *Homo Viator*, trans. E. Crauford (New York: Harper, 1962).

MB, I *The Mystery of Being*, vol. 1, trans. G. S. Fraser (South Bend: St. Augustine's Press, 2001).

MB, II *The Mystery of Being*, vol 2, trans. R. Hague (South Bend: St. Augustine's Press, 2001).

ME, I & II *Le Mystère de L'Être* (Paris: Aubier, 1951).

MJ *Metaphysical Journal*, trans. B. Wall (Chicago: Gateway, 1952).

PE *The Philosophy of Existentialism*, trans. M. Harari (New York: Citadel, 1962).

PI *Presence and Immortality*, trans. M. Machado (Pittsburgh: Duquesne University Press, 1967).

TW *Tragic Wisdom and Beyond*, trans. S. Jolin and P. McCormick (Evanston: Northwestern University Press, 1973).

Full information on these works is given in the bibliography.

COMMENTARY ON VOLUME ONE:

REFLECTION AND MYSTERY

I

INTRODUCTION

In his first chapter Marcel introduces his readers to his conception of philosophy and thereby indicates how we should approach this work. He also discusses the kind of audience his book is intended for and that entails an analysis of the kind of truth that is available in philosophy.

Marcel begins [I, 1-2] by stating that he has no intention of attempting to present his own philosophical "system" and showing its superiority over all others. That is an interesting comment since he tells us elsewhere[1] that when he began his philosophical studies his initial goal was to construct his own organized conceptual system which would start with truths known to be absolutely certain and step by logical step deduce from them further truths. Such a system would be designed to, at least in general, explain the whole of reality by means of rigorously interconnected propositions. (A model of such a system could be found in Spinoza's *Ethics* and Hegel's *Logic*, perhaps even in Euclid's *Elements of Geometry*.)

Marcel advances a number of reasons why, even as a young man, he came to reject that ideal.[2] For one thing, he found that he could not integrate into a supposedly universal and necessary system his own particular experiences with all their uniqueness and gaps [I, 3]. For another, he came to realize that the presumption that reality as a whole could be captured in logical propositions by any one thinker was absurd if not arrogant. In addition, the idea that he or anyone could offer their *own* philosophical system as if it were their private property ignores the fact that no one can know with any precision all the intellectual influences which have entered into his or her thought, nor what, if anything, is original.[3]

Instead of system building, Marcel describes philosophy as an "aid to discovery," a quest, "a search for or investigation into the essence of spiritual reality" [I, 1-2]. Of course, that means that *The Mystery of*

---

1   CF, 14, 60.

2   CF, 14-15.

3   CF, 60-61.

Being is intended to aid those who read it to discover and investigate the essence of spiritual reality. (What he means by spiritual reality will become clear as we proceed.) Similarly, in *The Existential Background of Human Dignity*,[4] he describes the philosopher as like an explorer in an unknown land or a walker in a new neighborhood who does not have a precise object in mind—as does a prospector or technician. Because the philosopher is free *[I, 15]* from preconceived notions or prejudices about what to expect, everything he or she comes across can be welcomed and enjoyed as a gift, nothing is dismissed as irrelevant. In *Creative Fidelity*, he says that philosophers should be like preschool children who wonder about, and are receptive to, everything they encounter because their experience of reality is fresh and alive, not encrusted over by dead habits.[5] Needless to say, given his conception of philosophy as an open ended search rather than an attempt to construct an all inclusive conceptual system of rationally connected truths, it is not surprising that in his philosophical works Marcel often appears to wander from one topic to another.

We must not exaggerate that, however, for he also indicates that he will follow an orderly procedure in these Gifford lectures since he will use them as an opportunity to review his work, his research, from a fresh perspective and point out its "general direction" and the interconnection ("joints," "hinges," and "articulations") of its various features *[I, 3]*. As a result *The Mystery of Being* does in fact provide an "approximate synthesis" of his journey, he affirms elsewhere.[6]

Perhaps equally important, he believes a review of his explorations can help others find and walk the road of discovery he has traveled, a winding road whose destination is not known beforehand *[I, 3-6]*. Every authentic philosopher must personally walk that road, he insists. Unlike the technician and engineer who can use methods of discovery and production invented by others and who do not have to repeat their original experiments, each philosopher must individually be "involved" in *[I, 8]* and "gripped by"[7] a philosophical question, no matter how ancient it may be, and seek to respond personally to it. I believe this is what he means by stating that "between a philosophical investigation and its

---

4   EBHD, 81-90.

5   CF, 11-12.

6   EBHD, 3.

7   CF, 63.

final outcome, there exists a link which cannot be broken" [I, 5]. The philosopher cannot simply accept the results of others' thoughts and build on them. (Needless to say, that means that anyone now reading his work must become personally involved in the questions and search for answers that Marcel himself engages in.)

It follows that philosophical truths cannot be "lost in anonymity" as technical and scientific discoveries can. In science, at least in its applied not theoretical side, where the difference between science and technology "reaches a vanishing point" [I, 6], one can build upon truths established by others without retracing their steps. This is because such truths are in principle universal, Marcel says, by which he means they can be demonstrated by any one who can use the proper tools or method [I, 7]. For example, anyone can show that water is composed of two parts hydrogen and one part oxygen, provided he or she can perform the proper laboratory experiment. Indeed, the chemist can simply take it as established that water is H_2O and move on without repeating the experiment and without even knowing exactly how or by whom that truth was first discovered.

However, if philosophical truth is not universally valid for anyone and everyone, if it must be the fruit of a personal inquiry by each individual philosopher, does this mean, Marcel asks, that such truth is purely subjective; that is, valid only for the particular individual who discovers and enunciates it? [I, 8-9] He answers that between the two alternatives, universal and purely individual, there is "an intermediate type of thinking" [I, 9] in which philosophy engages and he offers as an example of it the thinking that is involved in the appreciation of great works of art. While not everyone is sensitive to a musical masterpiece such as the *Missa Solemnis* or a great painting such as Van Gogh's Sunflowers, the recognition of their beauty is not a purely individual or private matter either [I, 9-10]. The beauty of works of art can be revealed to many, at least to all who have a properly cultivated ear or eye. Similarly, philosophical truths are not accessible universally, that is, by absolutely everyone, but by all those who have "a certain kind of aptitude" [I, 14] or certain dispositions, and Marcel mentions the following. A philosopher must not insist that the sole purpose of knowledge is its practical results [I, 4, 7]. The "point of departure" for a philosopher is a feeling of "metaphysical unease" [I, 7] or "anxiety"[8] which elsewhere he calls a "wonder which tends to become disquiet" about the human being's "fundamental situa-

8   EBHD, 10-16.

tion" in the world and about "reality as a whole."[9] "It consists above all," he writes, "in not taking reality for granted."[10] Philosophers are gripped by the most ultimate questions—"Why do I exist?", "Is there meaning to human life?", "Is there a God?", "What is truth?", etc. They experience an "intellectual demand" *[I, 7]*[11] for the spiritual illumination of truth *[I, 13]* in order to answer to some degree those fundamental questions. Because they seek *ultimate* truths, philosophers are distinguished "by the level at which they make their demands on life," he says *[I, 14]*. Note, in passing, that Marcel does not use the term philosopher to refer primarily to professional thinkers or academics, or even writers like himself. Every person who has the aforementioned unease or anxiety about the ultimate mysteries of life and who feels a deep inner demand to try and understand them is considered a philosopher by him.[12] He also describes the philosopher as someone who asks "true questions" namely, questions "which point to a line of direction along which we must move ... to get more and more chance of being visited by a sort of spiritual illumination" from the spiritual light which is truth *[I, 13]*. Obviously, that statement and metaphor need more explanation and he will devote all of Chapter 4 to a discussion of truth. For now, let us recall that he already stated that he intends in these lectures to indicate the general direction of the philosophical road he has traveled in order to aid others to join him. No doubt that is a road on which he believes he has experienced some illuminations from the spiritual light of truth, illuminations which he hopes to assist others in receiving.

In concluding my explication of this first chapter, I want to simply note something Marcel mentions at the very beginning but does not develop. He states there that he felt it necessary to respond to the "call" to give the Gifford lectures and, had he rejected the invitation, he would have felt guilty of "an indefensible betrayal" *[I, 2]*. By those remarks he briefly introduces an idea very important to him, that of a call or vocation, a topic he will discuss later, especially in Chapter 7. Even now, we have seen that he considers the philosopher to be some

---

9   TW, 6; EBHD, 12.

10   TW, 6. Also, EBHD, 13.

11   The French word is *exigence* (ME, I, 20, 22, et. al.) which is stronger than need; I will translate it either as demand or exigency. See the translator's note, MB, I, 39, and my note 1, page 25 of this commentary.

12   In TW, 9-10, he makes this very clear.

one who responds to a call or vocation to seek ultimate truths, or, in his metaphorical language, to seek illumination by the spiritual light which is truth.

Pages in other works of Marcel that treat material in this chapter:

CF, 7, 11-15, 58-65   EBHD, Chapters 1 and 2.

TW, 3-11; Chapter 2.   MJ, vii-viii, xi-xiii.

2

THE BROKEN WORLD

At the beginning of this chapter, Marcel returns to some of the issues about truth that he raised in Chapter 1. He repeats his criticism of the notion that truth must be something "universally valid," that is, "true for anybody and everybody" [I, 18] for, he says, that presupposes that there is a universal method or technique (for example, the scientific or experimental method) that can be used by anybody and everybody to obtain a desired result, in this case, truth [I, 19-20]. Perhaps his point will be clearer if we insert here his definition of technique in *Man Against Mass Society*.[1] A technique, he states, is a group of procedures capable of being taught and reproduced, designed to achieve some concrete goal by manipulating physical or mental objects. Now to believe that the right technique will produce truth, Marcel states, imagines truth to be a "thing" [I, 19], a "content," or a "formula" [I, 20] that in principle can be found by anyone who uses the correct set of procedures. Yet, the more we go beyond the purely technical realm, the realm of reproducible procedures designed to manipulate objects, the less the notion of a technique usable by anybody to produce truth valid for everybody applies. What sense would it make to say, for example, that the truths of Einstein's theories of relativity or of Aquinas' proofs of God's existence could have been obtained by anyone who adopted the correct techniques of manipulation? Truth is not reducible to a formula produced by the manipulation of mathematical or linguistic symbols. Rather, to understand a truth is to have an insight into the intelligible content of some reality—a content which can be expressed by many different symbols. Furthermore, I cannot represent materially the process by which I attain that insight and achieve an understanding of some thing [I, 20]. Instead of pursuing these points here, however, Marcel returns to the dispositions necessary for philosophical research and discusses at length the features of our culture (a culture enamored of technology) that pose obstacles for those dispositions and that research.

---

1 MAMS, 82, 251. This work contains Marcel's most extensive critique of Western society and its obsession with techniques.

He repeats from Chapter 1 his description of the philosopher as someone who has "an unusual sense of inner urgent demand" [I, 21][2] to ask the most fundamental questions about human existence and reality as a whole and to seek answers for them. Unfortunately, the tremendous technical progress in our time has led to a systematic misunderstanding and even discrediting of that demand, Marcel complains, and that is because technical progress is taken as an end in itself and so is freed from questions about what goals or values it should serve. In *Man Against Mass Society*, Marcel observes that in our culture technical progress seems to many to be the necessary and infallible way to obtain human well being and happiness, and the latter is identified with pleasure and satisfaction on a material level—for example, the accumulation of more and more amusements and possessions.[3] As a result, the need for, and joys of, a rich spiritual life, a life dedicated to intellectual and moral virtues, to love, beauty, truth and justice, tends to be downplayed and ignored. That materialistic mentality, which he calls "the spirit of technology,"[4] assumes that correct techniques can solve all human problems from birth to death, or, if they can't, the problems are simply meaningless. The consequence of this mentality, Marcel contends, is a "broken world" [I, 22], quoting from his play of the same name, "a world divided" and "at war with itself" [I, 23], with no heart, like a watch with no spring (or battery).

One of the most obvious reasons for the brokenness of our world and the anguish or, at least, the uneasiness that accompanies it is the possibility of world wide war resulting in the destruction of the human race. Such suicide is conceivable because among the fruits of our amazing technological progress are weapons of mass destruction possessed by many states whose relationships with each other are primarily in terms of power, often blatantly manifest in the desire for conquest [I, 23-24]. In an interesting move, Marcel goes on to link his notion of the broken world and the view that technical progress is an end in itself with what he designates as the "will to power" [I, 24], the conception of the ultimate nature of reality advanced by the nineteenth century philosopher Frederich Nietzsche. He quotes a passage from Nietzsche's

─────────────

2   Again the word in French is *exigence* (ME, I, 28) which is stronger than need.

3   MAMS, 55-57, 95.

4   MAMS, 97.

work *The Will to Power* which asserts that the world and everything in
it, including human beings, is a will or drive for power, a "monster of
energy"*[I, 25]* "and nothing else" *[I, 26]*. But to conceive of reality as
nothing but power, he points out, means that there is nothing beyond
power which could dominate or even grasp it *[I, 27]*. That is reflected
today, he says, in the fact that people are so fascinated by the power of
human technology that they make it an end in itself and are unwilling
to subject it to any values, even the value of truth. Of course to reject the
value of truth, he notes, logically undermines the alleged truth of every
world view including Nietzsche's that reality is nothing but the will to
power. Indeed, the irreconcilability of the will to power and the will to
truth is itself one manifestation of our broken world, he adds *[I, 27]*.
He also very briefly suggests that the fascination with power is behind
the atheism of our day. In *Man Against Mass Society* he explains what
he means by stating that human beings today are idolaters of themselves because of their power to shape the world, including themselves,
and so refuse to acknowledge or even consider their dependence on a
Creator.[5]

As for defining the broken world, Marcel characterizes it as one in
which people tend to become isolated atoms so that "the idea of any real
community becomes more and more inconceivable." "The very idea of a
close human relationship [or] intimate relationship...is becoming increasingly hard to put into practice and is even being rather disparaged" *[I,
28]*. That is because of the depersonalization of men and women which
results from the increased use of techniques which transform society
into complex bureaucratic organizations *[I, 28-31]*. Earlier we noted
that Marcel defines techniques as procedures designed to achieve goals
by manipulating objects. Now if techniques of manipulation are applied
to social organizations, they become bureaucracies in which everyone
must be stripped down to a set of functional categories and registered
on an official dossier so that those in power may efficiently organize and
control them to attain desired goals. (And those who have the power to
manipulate others may be viewed as almost godlike, especially if they
control the very necessities of life *[I, 32]*.) As a consequence, human
beings become what he calls "abstract individuals" *[I, 29]* for they are
reduced to agents whose "behavior ought to contribute towards the
progress of a certain social whole" *[I, 28]*. In other words, people are
identified with the socially useful functions they perform— one is a

5   MAMS, 62-68, 75.

bus driver or a teacher or a welder, period.[6] In addition, in order to make them more manageable, many functions themselves are reduced to abstract, uncreative, unchallenging, narrowly specialized tasks designed to eliminate any diversity arising from an individual's unique skills or talents. (Think of the traditional assembly line or the modern office composed primarily of data entry clerks.) Let me add that since machines are more easily controlled than human beings, human skills are increasingly built into them leaving the individual worker only the repetitive and mind deadening tasks of machine serving and tending.

Marcel concedes that in such a "bureaucratized world," where people relate to each other primarily as functions, a certain kind of social equality could exist among them [I, 31]. In *Man Against Mass Society* he identifies equality with the feeling that one is just as good and has the same rights as everyone else.[7] That kind of equality can only be "obtained by leveling down" [I, 31], he explains, because such equality ultimately means "sameness;"[8] to say that I am your equal is to maintain that I am the same as you. But given the obvious differences among human beings (in physical prowess, intellectual ability, artistic creativity, and so forth), an equality which is equated with sameness can be obtained only at a minimal level where all significant differences among people are eliminated—and to the extent that differences cannot be eliminated resentment is very likely, he adds [I, 32].

Relations which emphasize equality are very different from those of fraternity, he argues.[9] The latter implies the idea of a common father (or parent), in particular of a transcendent Being who has created and loved each unique person [I, 31-32]. Without the intimate ties of brotherhood (and sisterhood) among human beings who share a common father, Marcel says, the prevailing tendency of society is toward social atomization, where, as noted above, individuals see themselves and are seen as isolated atoms united only externally by a powerful elite and "subordinated to definite materialistic purposes" [I, 32], such as

---

6   See *MB, II*, 37-40.

7   MAMS, 208-09.

8   MAMS, 27.

9   Although he uses the traditional term fraternity, I am sure he is not referring only to relations between males.

the production and consumption of commodities. The image for that highly organized but broken world is, "a sort of ant hill" *[I, 24]*.

Now in speaking of our world as broken, Marcel makes it clear that he does not mean to imply that a break has occurred only in recent years; after all, doesn't the theological dogma of original sin mean that the world was always broken *[I, 34]*? Nor does he mean to suggest that every society today is thoroughly broken for there still remains something within human beings that protests against total atomism and total dehumanization *[I, 33]*. What we can say, he believes, is that the broken state of our world has become more obvious today *[I, 34]* for, unlike people of earlier times, we do not live in an age of optimism but rather one of "widely diffused pessimism" in which life itself tends to be considered almost "as a dirty joke."[10] Such pessimism is the result of despair, a despair which is inevitable if people put all their faith in techniques, since techniques are powerless to deal with the most fundamental questions about the meaning of life and death. As for death, from a technical point of view, the logical response to it is simply to scrap what is no longer of any use.[11]

Marcel concludes this chapter by restating why he has gone into these topics. He explains again that he felt it necessary to describe the conditions of our day which make philosophical investigations very difficult *[I, 35]*. Those conditions, such as an excessive reliance on techniques to solve all problems, lead to devaluing or even ignoring the urgent human demand which prompts a person to philosophize, that is, to seek ultimate truths about the meaning of human existence and of reality as a whole.

Our broken world, he adds, where self-destruction is possible, rests on an immense refusal to reflect (for example, on the purpose and effects of all our techniques) and imagine (for example, the horrendous effect of a nuclear holocaust or the abysmal poverty of much of the human race). And the refusal to reflect and imagine is the result of the grip that desire and fear and vanity have on men today *[I, 36-37]*. Although he does not amplify those remarks, I would suggest, in light of the topics just discussed, that he is probably referring to our *desire* to technically manipulate everything (including human beings) in order to produce and possess all those *desirable* material goods that promise happiness,

---

10   MAMS, 57.

11   MAMS, 94-97; CA, 174.

the *fear* of losing control of our techniques, leading in the worst case scenario to self-destruction, and the *vanity* "of specialists, those who set themselves up as experts" *[I, 37]*. He specifically mentions so-called experts in the field of education, but I think we could speak generally of the widespread vanity of human beings who think and live as though they are the creators of themselves and their world.

Of course, reflection is absolutely necessary when undertaking any task and that includes philosophy for, as we shall see later, the philosophical search essentially involves a certain kind of reflection. For now, Marcel ends the lecture by suggesting that when reflection seeks to become transparent to itself about its essential nature, it will come to see that it bases itself on something not itself, namely, an "intuition ... of supra-reflective unity" from which it draws its strength and its ability to critique itself *[I, 38]*. Needless to say, at this early stage of his investigation, those final brief remarks are extremely obscure. Fortunately, in Chapter 5 he will undertake an extensive discussion of the nature of reflection and its basis.

Pages in other works of Marcel that treat material of this chapter:
MAMS, Part I, Chapter 3, Part II, Chapter 5.
TW, 12-15.   CA, 172-75.   MB, II, 42-45.

3
THE EXIGENCY[1] FOR TRANSCENDENCE

Marcel devotes a good portion of this chapter to discussing the urgent inner demand which is the source and impetus for philosophy. In Chapter 1 that exigency was described as a demand for understanding which would alleviate the metaphysical uneasiness or anxiety about one's fundamental situation in the world. Here in Chapter 3, he immediately calls the inner exigency "a demand for transcendence" [I, 39] and states that it involves a certain "kind of dissatisfaction" which can be found both in myself and in all those whose "inner attitude" I can sympathize with [I, 42]. In the course of his inquiry into the meaning of transcendence, he also sets forth his views about the nature of human experience and knowledge and, in doing so, offers his first description of his philosophical procedure.

As for transcendence, Marcel states first that it cannot mean merely "going beyond" a spatial or temporal boundary. He intends, he says, to use the term in contrast to the immanent and "as it is presented to us in textbooks of metaphysics and theology" [I, 39]. However, since he neglects to specify which among the many different textbooks he has in mind, we will have to determine the meaning(s) he gives the term as he proceeds.

After suggesting in passing that there are a horizontal and a vertical transcendence, and defending his use of spatial metaphors in philosophy [I, 39-41] (for we are incarnate beings and in our experience our bodily postures correspond to certain emotions—such as feeling low or high), Marcel begins a discussion of two types of transcendence by reflecting upon easily recognizable concrete examples of going beyond or transcending certain dissatisfying situations. (Later in this volume [I, 116], he explains that in his philosophical approach "the use of examples ... [is] an essential part of our method of progressing." An example, he says, is

---

1 The translator's footnote on I, 39, points out that the French word *exigence* is stronger than the English word need. Even more important, Marcel himself in Volume II [II, 37] states that *exigence* should not be translated as need and suggests the word demand. Accordingly, I will translate *exigence* either as demand or as the English cognate exigency.

like fertile soil in which ideas are like planted seeds and one must keep
watch on the soil in order to see what the seed grows into, that is, to
understand the ideas embodied in the example.) His first example is of
a person who is dissatisfied with the deficiencies of her present situation
and seeks certain *external* goods, such as money or power, in order to
go beyond those deficiencies *[I, 42-43]*. The second, which he believes
involves the true exigency for transcendence, is a person who yearns for
an *inner* transformation, for example, to be more creative or more holy
[I, 44]. His best illustration of the second is the inner transformation
of a husband who radically changes his attitude towards his wife from
considering her only as someone who serves him to seeing her as someone
who exists in her own right with intrinsic value *[I, 48]*. That involves a
change in the very mode of his experience, Marcel says, a transformation in his fundamental attitude and actions toward others and toward
himself, and he adds that such a transformation is not simply due to
one's own will for it involves responding to one's vocation *[I, 44]* and
creating oneself *"above* oneself" *[I, 45]*, that is, creating oneself beyond
what he or she is at present. The fulfillment of one's vocation, he says,
"involves a cooperation from a whole swarm of conditions over which
the person with the vocation has no direct control" *[I, 44]*.[2]

As I mentioned above, in the course of discussing the exigency for
transcendence, Marcel also engages in a rather extensive treatment of
a number of related and important issues about the nature of human
experience and knowledge, and talks about his own philosophical
method. I will begin with the latter. In this chapter *[I, 47, 57]* and in
many other places, he states that his procedure can be characterized as
phenomenological.[3] That is, his method is to reflect upon and describe
features of life as we "concretely live" and experience them *[I, 41]*. By
carefully describing our ordinary life experiences or "lived experiences"
[I, 41, 46], we will be able to grasp their essential features, or, as he
graphically puts it, to "map out" or "outline [their] shape." Such map-
ping, which must always be faithful to what is revealed in experience,
can help us understand ("throw more light on") life itself. In other
works, Marcel emphasizes that philosophy is not an attempt to move
away from experience into a realm of pure thought but is a "digging" or
"drilling" into ordinary human experience which "provides the means

---

2   This statement refers to his notion of the situation which he will discuss
in Chapter 7.

3   Some other places in this volume are: *60, 88-90, 94, 106*.

for experience to become aware of itself, to apprehend itself"[4] so deeply that we become aware of the "secret powers" which are its source and nourishment.[5] Thus experience "is not so much a springboard but a promised land"[6] for it is only *within* experience, not beyond it, that we will come to understand ourselves and our world and discover the secret powers which will, to some degree, satisfy our urgent inner demand for transcendence. Perhaps Marcel is also referring to those secret powers when he asserts that a "certain character of transcendence" can be found in "the rawest and most familiar reality" we experience [I, 45].

However, isn't it self-contradictory to suggest that we can find *within* experience that which to some degree satisfies our demand for *transcendence?* To think that way, he replies, is to have "far too restrictive an idea of experience" [I, 47], one "which robs experience of its true nature" [I, 55]. It is to imagine experience to be a kind of physical substance and the transcendent to be beyond and outside of that substance. But, Marcel says, if we "reflect upon what experience really is" [I, 46], in other words, if we look at experience as we live it, we see that experience is not an object, meaning some thing or substance that can be "placed before me," for I cannot separate my experience from myself. Furthermore, to speak of some thing *outside* of my experience (transcendent in that sense) is meaningless for I could judge something to be outside of experience only "*from within* experience" [I, 46]. If something is really outside of or beyond experience, it is, he points out, beyond what can be thought or felt and so there is no way I could even be aware of it [I, 47-48]. Thus, he concludes, the word transcendent does "*not* mean 'transcending experience,' but on the contrary there must exist a possibility of having an experience *of* the transcendent as such" [I, 46]; otherwise the word is meaningless.

If one continues to insist that the term transcendence means that which is absolutely other, which by definition must fall outside experience, that presupposes, Marcel claims, that "all experience in the end comes down to a self's experience of its own internal states" [I, 49]. That views experience as a matter of "ingesting" or taking in something [I, 47], such as images, stimuli, or ideas and, once again, visualizes consciousness as

---

4   CF, 14-15.

5   TW, 14.

6   "An Essay in Autobiography" in PE, 106.

a bodily container inside of which are various "states." He attacks this position in a variety of ways.

For one thing, he argues that the very notion of a "state of consciousness" is questionable since consciousness "cannot be considered as a body" for, he affirms, he agrees with Descartes (and the idealism derived from him) who insisted that consciousness is "essentially something that is the contrary of a body, of a thing" [I, 50].[7] (However, he does not indicate which, if any, of Descartes' particular arguments he accepts.)[8] Marcel contends that while it is clear that any body is capable of undergoing all kinds of successive modifications or changes of states or representations, consciousness *itself* is not. "Itself" is the key word, he says, for to speak of a self is to refer to something permanent [I, 51]. To illustrate, I am now in some sense the *same* self I was at age 6 and age 50. I experience my self having many different experiences and performing many different activities in the course of my life and yet persisting as the same me through them all. Now, every body, including mine, constantly and thoroughly changes, especially at the cellular and molecular levels. Since there is nothing permanent in my body, Marcel concludes, it cannot strictly speaking be a self. (Let me add, that if a body is not permanent, neither would be its representations or states.)

Furthermore, when we refer to consciousness as if it were an object like a body, we are thinking of ourselves as outside of it but, as pointed out earlier in reference to our experience, we cannot really detach or separate ourselves from our consciousness and view it as an external object. Therefore, Marcel reasons, any position (like Spinoza's) that claims that consciousness is "simply bodily states looking at themselves or becoming objects for themselves" must also be rejected [I, 51][9]

---

7   Recall that on his very first page Marcel said that these lectures were a search for, or investigation into, spiritual reality. We now see that both the conscious self and its experience are spiritual realities for him.

8   On I, 49 he contrasts Descartes and idealists who give priority to the thinking self from empiricists like Hume who reduce the self to nothing but a nonsubstantial collection of states. Marcel's most detailed discussion of the nature of the self will be later in Chapter 9.

9   Marcel says Spinoza held that the mind is the "representation" or idea of the body, and that states of consciousness are nothing but images (representations, therefore) of the body's states. Since the conscious state or representation mirrors the state of the body, it is in a sense the way "a body looks at itself." He also refers to that position as "psycho-physical parallelism," I, 51.

If, instead of imagining ourselves outside of consciousness, we reflect upon our conscious experience as we live it, we will see that Husserl's phenomenology is correct when it asserts that "before it is anything else consciousness is conscious of something other than itself" and not of its own internal states [I, 52]. For example, when I am conscious of the tree in my backyard ten feet from my garage, I do not—as in the ingestion view of experience and knowledge—bring the tree or its image into my mind. Rather, I am present in my experience to that tree right where it is in my backyard. To claim otherwise, that I know only objects *within* my consciousness, Marcel asserts in an earlier work, is to deny our most basic spontaneous experience—something no one who proceeds phenomenologically would ever do. In *Being and Having* he writes, "A philosophy which denies I can know anything except what it calls my 'states of consciousness' is shown to be clearly false when we confront it with the spontaneous and irresistible affirmation which forms as it were the ground-base of human knowledge."[10] Of course, my "spontaneous and irresistible affirmation" is that the tree I know and experience in my backyard is indeed in my backyard—not within my consciousness. In fact, that I experience real things in the world is my most "certain [and] intimate experience," he insists, and it is a mere "academic" exercise to deny it.[11] Indeed, such a denial expresses "contempt" for the evidence of experience.[12]

In the lengthy quotation above, Marcel refers to the experience of things other than the self as the "ground-base of human knowledge" which means that any reflective consciousness of one's own self and its states is a "derivative act" [I, 52] rooted in that basic experience. His point is that in order to become conscious of my self and my conscious acts by reflection, I must first of all be nonreflectively directly conscious of things other than the self, else I have nothing to reflect upon. And, just as my basic nonreflective acts pass beyond or transcend my self by being aware of things in the world, so too, he states, my reflective acts of self-awareness pass beyond or transcend the self which I reflect upon—and this characteristic of consciousness, its "passing beyond," he asserts, "is enough in itself to dispose of the idea of consciousness as a mere mirror" of the body [I, 52].

---

10   BH, 54.

11   "An Essay in Autobiography" in PE, 117.

12   BH, 56.

I must confess I do not understand just what Marcel's argument is here. For him to speak of the reflecting consciousness passing beyond or transcending the reflected on consciousness is misleading since the self which reflects and the self reflected on are not two selves, he insists later, but different features of "a single lived reality" [I, 61]. Perhaps a clue to what he has in mind is that he seems to identify the view that consciousness is a mere mirror or representation of the body with epi-phenomenalism, a position which claims that consciousness is a "mere surface encrustation on matter" [I, 52]. Epiphenomenalism considers consciousness to be nothing but an effect or by product (epiphenomenon) of the brain's acts and, accordingly, to be a purely *passive* phenomenon produced by the brain. That means that one's conscious thoughts, choices, and desires have no power to cause or modify any of one's bodily activi-ties. Marcel's argument, then, may be that consciousness can't simply be a passive product of the body or its brain for, in becoming aware of itself, consciousness *actively* passes beyond or transcends the self it is aware of. Furthermore, if consciousness were no more than a passive mirror or surface encrustation of the body, it would be hard to see how it could be aware of things other than its body.

Toward the end of the lecture, Marcel reaffirms his emphasis on experience. One of the things that gets in our way, he says, is language, in particular the metaphors which refer to conscious acts as "grasping" or "seizing" or "gathering or taking" [I, 53] an object. Such terminology naturally lends itself to the ingestion view of experience and knowledge and so is especially inappropriate to describe the experience of discover-ing an "intelligible relation," for example, the truth of the principle of contradiction. An experience of that kind does not involve grasping something, he declares, but being illuminated or achieving "sudden access to some reality's revelation of itself to us" [I, 53]. No doubt, in order to communicate our insights or illuminations we need to put them into language and that brings with it the danger of "the expression of the illumination growing over the illumination ... and gradually taking its place" by claiming a " kind of independence" [I, 53] from the experience it is meant to signify. To avoid this, Marcel advises, we must continu-ally return to what is really present in experience. "There is no more important undertaking," he asserts, "than that of reinstating experience in the place of such bad substitutes for it" [I, 54].

Now what, he asks, is the relationship between his stress on experi-ence and the urgent inner demand for transcendence that he discussed earlier in this lecture? In response he refers to what he said earlier, transcendence does not refer to something beyond experience *[I, 54]* and so philosophy should not attempt to move away from experience but to enter more deeply into it. Therefore, the impetus for philosophy, the exigency for transcendence, must be a demand for a certain kind of experience. He proposes that it is an aspiration for "a purer and purer mode of experience," one that is open, free from prejudice, and receptive, and at the same time an aspiration for an experience of plenitude or fullness, which he cryptically links to the presence in experience of "imponderable elements" which he calls "intelligible essences" *[I, 55-56]*. Although he offers no illustration of such essences, I believe he referred to them above when he spoke about an "intelligible relation" being suddenly revealed to someone *[I, 53]*—as, for example, when a person recognizes the eternal truth that a plane triangle must have the sum of its interior angles equal to a straight line or, a particularly Marcellian theme, when we understand the difference between an I-him/her relation and an I-thou relation. Thus, for Marcel the urgent inner demand for transcendence is an urgent aspiration for a mode of experience which would be pure, that is, open and receptive, and at the same time full of intelligibility. Note that this description is similar to his earlier description, in Chapter 1, of the inner demand which gives rise to philosophy. That demand too was characterized as an *intellectual* exigency, a demand for intelligibility and truth about the fundamental mysteries of human existence.

Marcel ends the lecture by repeating his rejection of the view that to know is for the mind to be filled with a certain content like a vessel *[I, 56]*. Intelligence cannot be compared to a content, he says again, and we shall become even more convinced of that by going deeply into the notion of truth.

Pages in other works that treat material in this chapter:
CF, 14-15, 164-65.   MAMS, 22-25.
BH, 54-56.   PE, 106, 117.

4

TRUTH AS A VALUE:
THE INTELLIGIBLE MILIEU[1]

The fourth lecture is devoted to the topic of truth. It is very important to note at the outset that, as the title indicates, Marcel intends to investigate truth as a *value*, as, for example, when one is said to love truth or to sacrifice oneself for it. The traditional definition of truth as "the adequation [i.e. conformity] of the thing and the intellect" *[I, 58]*—meaning that a judgment in the intellect is true if it conforms to the way reality is—may have a theoretic value, he grants, but, surely, no one ever died for that abstract formula. Again, in order for someone to live or die for truth it must be experienced as possessing value.

Probably because many philosophers have traditionally identified truth with reality, Marcel first briefly discusses the relation between them. From a certain point of view there may be no difference, but he is interested in truth as only a single aspect of reality,[2] the latter being in essence "all inclusive" (quoting the English philosopher Bradley) *[I, 59]*. Besides, he says, the very idea of an all inclusive reality is questionable since at any given time an inclusive system of thought which *we* construct can never be totally complete because our future experiences have not been and cannot yet be included in it. Only if we claim to have somehow established ourselves beyond all temporal change and development, needless to say, an impossibility, could we possibly comprehend the all encompassing whole which reality is *[I, 59-60]*.

Rather than pursue these grand thoughts, however, let us, Marcel says, proceed more modestly as phenomenologists in order to investigate "the difference between *being* and *being true*" *[I, 60]*. In other words, let us reflect upon ordinary lived experience and see if we can find in it the aforementioned distinction. (It is very important to keep in mind

---

1   The French word is *milieu* and I believe it is more accurate to translate it straight forwardly as the English word milieu. That is the way the translator of Volume II renders it.

2   The English translation capitalizes the words truth and reality; the French text does not, ME, I, 69.

that in this chapter Marcel proceeds as a phenomenologist; that is, he *describes concrete human experiences* which involve truth. He does not attempt to conceptually analyze abstract notions of truth.)

After a brief excursion into the nature of sensation, a topic to which he will devote Chapter 6, Marcel gives examples from experience that illustrate the difference between reality and truth. A person can fall outside the bounds of truth, for example someone who does not admit he or she lacks a certain ability, and yet not outside the bounds of reality. On the other hand, someone can be within the bounds of truth and yet be suffering from a certain lack of reality, as, for example, a deaf person who admits his/her disability. In the latter case, the person "refuses to draw the blinds against a certain kind of light," he says, and he goes on to state that the metaphor of light can help us grasp the "essence of what we mean by truth" [I, 62]. In fact, he insists, to speak of truth as a light is not just an incidental metaphor but is part of the very texture of his argument for, after all, in ordinary language, which presumably arises from and expresses lived experience, we do speak of "blindness" to the truth or of being "dazzled" by it. To illustrate, he describes a person at the point of taking final vows to be a monk who has not faced the real reason, the facts, behind his choice of that vocation. He will not, we might say, "open himself to the light" [I, 63] or face the facts.

This takes Marcel into a rather extensive analysis of the nature of facts, or, more precisely, of how facts come to possess meaning and value—in his metaphorical language, how facts come to have the power to radiate light. In the first place, he says, facts are not something outside of me which have in themselves a certain meaning or which in themselves are a source of light. In themselves, facts are simply "inert, neutral element[s]" [I, 65] which take on meaning and value because of what a self or subject brings to them [I, 64-66]. We can use his example of the man who is at the point of taking final vows to illustrate his point. That a woman he loved refused his offer of marriage is simply a fact but what import it has on him depends on how he interprets it—and that depends on the kind of person he has become. If he is very religious, he might well consider his rejection as a sign God is calling him to the religious life. If he is a very self-confident individual, he probably would judge that she was unworthy of him anyway; if he is a hyper romantic, he might consider her his one true love and fall into despair. Clearly his interpretation depends on the perspective he brings, for it is through it that he evaluates the fact. Marcel puts it this way—the fact has the power to radiate light because it borrows that power from the subject, from what he calls its "living center" [I, 66]. He adds that the most concrete illustration of this living center would be found in a novel whose author described in some detail the surroundings in which a character, such as the would be monk, has lived and the influences they have exerted on him. That would enable the reader to understand the perspective of that character and thus why he reacts as he does to a disappointing romance.[3]

Another thing that Marcel says about the living center of a subject or self is that it is an essentially incomplete structure, since it exists in space and time and extends beyond our direct awareness of it [I, 67]. By that last remark I believe he is referring to all those aspects of myself, for example, many of my desires, aspirations, fears and memories, that I am not explicitly aware of at any given time. Since no self is an isolated monad shut in on itself but is continually affected by its human and natural environments in ways it is barely conscious of, Marcel goes so far as to state that its "uncompleted structure [extends] beyond the self" [I, 67], where by self I presume he means the conscious self.[4] Finally, he suggests that there is an intimate connection between the living structure of the self and its body. Although he will consider the relation between one's self and one's body in detail in the next chapter, let me just note that much of what Marcel has said here about the structure of the self can be said of my body. My body is constantly changing in space and time and most of its inner physiological operations go on beneath the level of my direct awareness as do many of my bodily actions on things in my environment as well as the effects of those things on my body.

He concludes these remarks by repeating his view that facts have value and meaning (the power to radiate light) only in reference to, or in some way "integrated into," the living incomplete structure of the self. If that structure is "swept away," the "idea of truth," namely, the meaning and value or radiance of facts, would "lose its meaning" [I, 67]. I will offer a final illustration of his point with reference to the body. Physical objects are factually just whatever they are. They possess no intrinsic meaning or value but take on meaningful features ("become radiant"),

3   Marcel refers also to the "unity" between a subject and its surroundings [I, 66], a topic he will discuss extensively when he presents his notion of the situation in Chapter 7.

4   I should also point out that the phrase "extends beyond itself" is not in the French edition, ME, I, 78.

become appetizing or dangerous or sexually attractive, for example, only in relation to the specific organic structure of the human body.

Of course, a particular self may or may not be disposed or receptive to the meaning or light which streams from the facts *[I, 67]*. To dispose oneself to that light the self must be willing to face the truth, that is, face the meaning or radiance of the facts. Marcel offers the helpful example of two parents who eventually come to face the painful truth that their child is abnormal. To do so involves both their activity of freely, courageously, opening themselves to that unpleasant truth and their willingness to accept and admit their child's deficiency. And, a real struggle may be involved in facing that truth, but, Marcel declares, the struggle is not against the truth or the fact of their child's abnormality but against themselves *[I, 69]*! There is an aspect of themselves which desires to avoid the painful admission and it struggles against another aspect of themselves which is willing to face the truth. He calls the latter the "spirit of truth" *[I, 69]* and elsewhere describes it as the willingness to dispose one's self to the light in order to see the true value of things.[5] (By the way, we are talking here about two different aspects of *one* self, Marcel insists, not two different selves *[I, 65, 69]*.)

Continuing with the light metaphor, Marcel writes, "in the light of truth I succeed in diminishing that permanent temptation ... to conceive reality, or to represent it to myself, as I should like it to be" *[I, 69]*. However, he immediately asks, does speaking of truth in that way mean that it is a "distinct power" or "substance" which can purify me if I open myself to it? That, he states, is "the essential question" *[I, 70]*. To pursue the point, he briefly refers to Martin Heidegger's lecture *On the Essence of Truth* in which the German philosopher refers to truth as a light that enables something to appear or be made manifest to us *as it is*, so that we can make true judgments about that thing, judgments that express it just as it has presented itself. Marcel affirms his fundamental agreement with Heidegger but repeats his question, can we treat the light of truth "as an effective power" *[I, 71]*?

Those questions remind him of his earlier statements about the love of truth, statements which also seem to make truth "an entity" *[I, 71]*. While the religious person might link the love of truth with the love of God, Marcel doubts that we can attribute a religious character to the love of truth present in an ordinary learned man or in a scientist. The latter might admit he passionately loves scientific research and has

5   HV, 140-41.

confidence in its social utility but he would not say that his love is of God [I, 72]. Yet suppose that a scientist loves truth so much that he is willing to be sent to a concentration camp rather than renounce the conclusions his research has led him to. Surely, he is not doing this to preserve his self-respect, for the scientist's experience is that "it is not *himself* that is at stake, but *truth*" [I, 72]; it is truth to which he witnesses and is unwilling to betray. But it would seem that we can only betray a person, so "is truth a person, can it be compared to a person?" he asks. Again the religious individual might respond affirmatively but Marcel is hesitant since we are excluding the world of religious experience here because the scientist is most likely a nonbeliever.

If we pursue the idea that truth can be compared to a person, perhaps, Marcel suggests, the American philosopher Josiah Royce is on to something when he says that those who search for truth enter into an ideal community or city of truth seekers who take joy in communicating with each other in their search. Betrayal of truth, then, would mean treason against that community [I, 73-74]. However, that still does not answer the question what truth itself is, for the ideal community of truth seekers draws "its very existence from that … light which is truth" [I, 74] and so that light is not the community itself. Rather, truth is what that community is striving towards and what animates its search.

That leads Marcel to remark that he has not yet asked exactly how tasks, in this case the task to search for truth, get suggested to thought in the first place [I, 75]. In other words, how does it happen that truth (or any other value) is experienced as something worthy of pursuit? However, rather than undertaking that inquiry at this time, he concludes the lecture by stating that all communication (including that between the members of a community of truth seekers) takes place within a realm of intersubjectivity (term to be defined later but for now we can say interpersonal relations), which he calls an "intelligible milieu" [I, 75]. Although he does not explain what he means by such a milieu, I believe his reference to intersubjectivity indicates that it is a community such as Royce envisioned made up of those presently united in their common search for truth and who take joy in communicating with each other in their quest. Love of truth, then, Marcel says, could in one sense be joy in being within that milieu and being outside the bounds of truth would mean falling outside that milieu [I, 75-76]. Looking ahead, he will claim in the next chapter that the milieu is also the "place" where truth may reveal itself and enlighten those who love and seek it. For now, he closes by stating that the intelligible milieu is not something to which we naturally or natively belong and that we gain access to it only under "rather difficult conditions" which he does not specify. That prompts him to turn in his next lecture to "the world we do naturally belong to, the world of our sense experience" [I, 76].

Thus Marcel ends this lecture without pursuing any further the nature of truth as a value or as a light which illuminates things and animates those who seek it. However, if we review what he has said here about truth and light, and supplement his remarks with relevant material from other works, we can, I believe, attain a more complete understanding of his views.

Both in this chapter and elsewhere, when discussing truth as light, Marcel distinguishes between what is illuminated, and so radiates light, from the light which is the source of that illumination and radiation. Since in this lecture he is considering truth as a value, I would suggest that his metaphor be understood as the distinction between truth as the value or significance of something and truth as the source of that meaning and value.[6] In one of his latest works, Marcel talks about the common experience of "coming to understand ... what was initially obscure to us" and says that when we do so, "light floods our minds."[7] That should remind us of his earlier remark that to suddenly recognize the validity (truth) of an intelligible relation, such as a mathematical proof, is "to have sudden access to a reality's revelation of itself to us" and "to be illuminated" [I, 53]. More generally, Marcel asserts that "illumination" accompanies "every act of genuine understanding"[8] which I take to mean every act of apprehending truth.

Now from the beginning of this chapter, he has said that he is investigating truth insofar as it is a value. I would suggest, then, that when he speaks of the experience of light flooding our minds or our experience of being illuminated when we gain access to something's self-revelation, he is usually talking about our experience or "genuine understanding" of some reality's *value*. In Chapter 3, he spoke about the husband who eventually comes to recognize the truth that his wife possesses value of

---

6   In *Searchings,* no trans. (New York: Newman Press, 1967), 20, Marcel speaks of the source of light which makes seeing possible and states that by seeing he means evaluating.

7   TW 14, 209. See also, MB, II, 120-21; EBHD, 86, 95; *Searchings,* 20.

8   TW, 211.

her own. In this fourth chapter, he referred to parents who after great
struggle acknowledge the truth that their child is abnormal and to the
scientist who refuses to betray truths that his research had discovered.
Elsewhere, he speaks of the recognition of truths about the dignity and
sacred value of human life.[9] In all of these cases, truth is experienced
by the individuals in question as the revelation or illumination of the
value of something or someone, a value they should recognize and
acknowledge even though to do so may cause them pain or great hardships. Marcel's recurring question is, what is truth that is the source
of those values experienced in the wife, in acknowledging the facts of
the child's condition, in the scientific result, in human life? And what
is the source of people's receptiveness to such values or, metaphorically,
of their receptiveness to the illumination of the light? What (power?)
purifies the husband, the parents, the scientist, those who recognize
the dignity of human life, so that they have the courage and strength to
overcome their desire to see things as they would like them to be and
instead open themselves to the light and acknowledge things as they
are?

Although he does not do so in this chapter, in other places Marcel
makes it clear that those who experience the radiance of light or the
truth or value of some things are not themselves the source of that
radiance.[10] Granted, as he discussed earlier in this chapter, things or
facts become radiant, they have value and meaning, only in relation to
the particular perspective or structure a human being brings to them.
Nevertheless, a perspective does not *create* the values it reveals. The
husband, the parents, and the scientist, for example, must be willing to
open themselves to the light, that is, to the truth about his wife, their
child, a scientific result, respectively. If they adopt the perspective of
open receptivity, certain truths will be illuminated and revealed to them,
namely, the wife's intrinsic value, the fact of the child's abnormality, the
scientifically verified results. In his metaphor, light will flood their minds.
And they will feel, not that they created those truths or values, but that
they have been revealed to them and that they have "an obligation" to

9   TW, 210; *Searchings*, 20.

10   TW, 209-12; PE, 87-88; MB, II, 120; MJ, xi. That may be what he means
in the present chapter by suggesting that the light of truth, while within us, is
also in some way "transcendent" [I, 70].

acknowledge and respond to them, even when it is hurtful or dangerous to do so *[I, 68]*.

Similarly, when Marcel states that it is *truth* that purifies individuals and so is the source of their openness to the light *[I, 70]*, he implies that those individuals themselves can not overcome their blindness and their desire to see things as they would like them to be. How could they on their own overcome their deficiencies; it would be like pulling themselves up by their own bootstraps. (In the previous chapter he made much the same point when he said one can't fulfill his or her high vocation without assistance for it involves creating oneself "above oneself" *[I, 44-45]*.) Furthermore, becoming more open may not be something that they themselves desire (at least on one level), especially if it would cause them great pain and adversity.

It is at this point that Marcel wonders if truth, then, is an entity or power which can purify us and also illuminate, that is, confer meaning and value on, things. Even more, he asks if truth could be a person, since it would seem that only a person could be loved or betrayed—as truth can be loved or betrayed. However, he does not pursue those provocative suggestions apparently because he fears that doing so may take him into the area of religion and as a philosopher he hesitates to go there. In Volume II of this work, we shall see that he is no longer reluctant to investigate various kinds of religious experiences and that doing so will indeed lead him ultimately to identify truth with the Person who is "the light of which St. John speaks as enlightening every man who comes into the world" *[II, 121]*.

Pages in other works that treat material in this chapter:
HV, 139-41.   MJ, xi.
MAMS, 70, 209-10.   *Searchings*, 16-20.
EBHD, 86-89, 95.   TW, 209-13.

5

PRIMARY AND SECONDARY REFLECTION: THE EXISTENTIAL REFERENCE POINT[1]

Marcel begins this lecture by stating that the intelligible milieu discussed in the previous chapter is the environment within which our philosophical research must take place. In other words, the community made up of persons animated by the love of truth who delight in communicating as they pursue that light is the "place" where truth may reveal itself by illuminating those who seek it. Of course, that community would include all who read Marcel and join with him on his winding path. Since he journeys as a philosopher and "philosophic thought ... is reflective" [I, 77], this naturally leads him into a discussion of the nature of reflection.

As usual Marcel begins with examples of reflection from ordinary experience or "the daily flow of life." In his first example, I reflect when I use my memory to retrace my earlier steps in order to find where I left my watch. In the second, I reflect when I question myself after I have told a lie to my friend. In the third, I reflect when I wonder about my right to judge others when I myself have behaved as badly as they [I, 78-80]. From these examples he draws the following conclusions. Reflection is a personal act that no one can do for another; it occurs when some obstacle or break interrupts the normal routine of my life and forces me to pay close attention to my experience; it occurs only when something valuable is at stake.

Before continuing his analysis of reflection, he pauses to address the objection that it stifles life and its vital impulses [I, 80-82]. Human life, Marcel responds, is more than biological functions or pure spontaneity like that of animals. For one thing, a purely biological account overlooks the fact that human life is always centered on some goal beyond itself. For another, to view life as mere spontaneity ignores the fact that reflection is an essential ingredient of *human* life, for in human beings life becomes aware of itself. Reflection is an integral and normal part of our complex human experience, he insists; it is "one of life's ways of

1   The French term is *repère* meaning a spatial landmark, benchmark, or reference point from which you take your bearings.

rising from one level to another" *[I, 82]*. That is, it transforms our life from something simply driven by passions and desires into a life lived by conscious choice and direction. Indeed, reflection is inevitable, he states, "experience cannot fail to transform itself into reflection" *[I, 83]*, apparently because, as mentioned, reflection naturally arises when some obstacle interrupts life's normal routine and one is forced to pay closer attention to his or her experience. Finally, reflection provides a "richness" of experience that would be missing if I lived without being aware of my thoughts, desires, feelings, choices, and other mental acts; in other words, if I lived without being aware of my inner self.

Now there are at least two types of reflection, Marcel claims, one he calls primary, the other secondary. The latter, he points out, has been present in these talks from the beginning since it is "the special high instrument of philosophical research" *[I, 83]*. Primary reflection, he states, "tends to dissolve the unity of experience which is first put before it" while secondary reflection "reconquers that unity." To illustrate the difference, he reflects on the reality of the self, or, more concretely, on the I who ask myself "who I am" and what I mean by "asking myself that question" *[I, 84]*.

Marcel's initial response to those questions is that he has a feeling of not being the one who is described in the various categories entered on an identity form, even though everything on that form is true of him. There seems to be, he notes, a "strange duality" *[I, 85]* between the definite somebody entered on the form and the self as a nonsomebody, a duality that appears as the result of reflection, apparently referring to primary reflection which dissolves the unity of the self given in experience. But, he states, we "have to go beyond" that duality and acknowledge that I *am* indeed a definite self, a particular individual or somebody, although I am not just that. In other words, paradoxically, I "appear to myself both as a somebody and not a somebody, a particular individual and not a particular individual" *[I, 86]*. Of course, to recognize that I am *both* involves secondary reflection which reconquers my experience of my self as *one* self with multiple dimensions.

Next, Marcel asks, can we "get a closer grip on this experience of the self as not being a somebody?" *[I, 86]*. We can, he answers, if we recognize that the experience in question is that the definite characteristics that make me a particular individual have a "contingent," that is, nonnecessary, character in relation to the "mysterious reality" which is "myself as subject" *[I, 87]*. That reality is my self which, strictly speaking, can never be an object for me even when I reflect on it, for I can not detach myself from my self in order to make my self an object external to me. (Recall his earlier definition of an object as something that can be placed before me *[I, 46]*.) The self as subject is the self "with whom I am intimate," he says, that traditionally has been felt to possess "a certain sacred reality" *[I, 87]*.

I would suggest that by the mysterious self as subject with whom I am intimate, the self that is not contingent, Marcel means that part of my self that I experience as me no matter how many different characteristics I gain or lose. I am now a particular individual who is a retired philosophy professor, a husband, father, Wisconsin resident, and more. And even when I was an engineering student, unmarried, California resident, I was still me, the unique person I have been since birth and will remain until death, no matter how many different features I acquire in the meantime. That persisting self is not contingent, meaning that I can never cease to be it and still be the unique person I am, and so it is most especially me, most especially the self "with whom I am intimate." It is mysterious because I never know precisely and exhaustively the subject I am, for I am always more than any characteristics I have and can describe.

Marcel then asks, does the self as subject *exist*? Surprisingly, his answer is negative—which is not to say the self is imaginary. The self as subject is "actual," he asserts, but strictly speaking does not exist, which, needless to say, requires him to undertake a discussion of the notion of existence. However, rather than attempt to define that term, he asks whether there is any existence that can serve as a touchstone or reference point of existence? That is, is there "some centrally significant existence" some "existential indubitable" that, were I to deny it, I could not assert the existence of anything else? Of course, he replies, that central existence is "myself in so far as I feel sure that I exist" *[I, 88]*.

Yet, to claim this, Marcel recognizes, is to risk a confrontation with total or modified skepticism. Total skepticism is not certain whether anything exists or what sort of thing could exist. Such a position, he points out, implies that I have a certain criterion of existence and that I am not sure if anything I experience satisfies that criterion. He quickly dismisses this position as meaningless from a phenomenological perspective, for in our ordinary human experience—and that, after all, is what phenomenology investigates—it is obvious that we distinguish between that which exists and that which does not *[I, 89]*.[2] Similarly, in his earliest work, *Metaphysical Journal*, Marcel asserts that, "unbiased reflection" on experience reveals that our most basic experience is of the existence of ourselves and the world.[3] Unless the mind, "deliberately sets aside" such experience, he insists, it "knows itself to be fortified by an unquestionable assurance of the existing universe."[4] "This assurance is of a global character," he explains, for "what is given to me beyond all possible doubt is the confused and global experience of the world inasmuch as it is existent."[5] As I read him, Marcel is not denying here that one can deliberately *in thought* set aside one's experience and *mentally* doubt the existence of the world. Many philosophers have done so. Rather he is stating that I cannot doubt that the existence of the world "is given to me" in my experience. In fact, it is the most fundamental given of my experience, the bedrock experience which is "the continuous foundation" of all my other experiences and knowledge.[6] I should add that he does not claim that the existence of any and every *particular* thing is indubitable. I can always be unsure whether an object of my experience is what I believe it to be, whether something I see through the fog is a tree or a human being, for example.[7] Nevertheless, even in those cases, I am sure that something exists.

He turns next to critique limited or relative skepticism, one that would question whether I myself exist *[I, 89]*. To even raise that question, he points out, is to treat myself as an object and make existence a predicate which may or may not be attributed to that object. (Note,

---

2   In his *Metaphysical Journal*, Marcel takes a different tack and makes the logical point that total skepticism self-destructs for if the skepticism is total than it must also be just as skeptical of any proposed criterion of existence (MJ, 320). The appendix to MJ remains one of his best treatments of existence, my body as mine, and sensation. I should add that in *MB, II, 2- 3*, Marcel states that many of the philosophical "solutions" that he first set forth in his early journals "do not differ fundamentally from those I shall put forward today."

3   MJ, 320-21.

4   MJ, 323.

5   MJ, 322.

6   F 165. My translation of "*base continue*", on 236 of *Essai de philosophie concrète* (originally published as *Du refus à l'invocation*), (Paris: Gallimard, 1966).

7   MJ, 322.

again, that the separation would be the activity of primary reflection.) On the contrary, my self is not and cannot be an object in the sense of something separate from me, nor is existence a predicate, he says, as Kant established once and for all. (Kant argued that existence is not a predicate because it adds no specific quality or content to any idea. His famous example is that there is no difference in meaning between 100 possible dollars and 100 real dollars; both are 100 dollars.) Rather than attributing a predicate "exists," to an object "I," the "I exist" must be treated as an "indissoluble unity," he contends, "the 'I' cannot be considered apart from the 'exist'" *[I, 90]*. Let me add that in his *Metaphysical Journal* Marcel makes exactly the same point about the existence of the world. Existence is not a predicate, he states there too, for "in reality existence and the thing that exists obviously cannot be dissociated."[8] Thus, the aforementioned "global assurance" of the existence of the world, "can only," he states, "bear on the indissoluble unity of existence and the existent."[9] (Of course, grasping that unity would be the activity of secondary reflection.)

In the same vein, here in *The Mystery of Being* Marcel also calls the relation between existence and the existent one of "pure immediacy" *[I, 90]*. By saying that, he wants to distinguish his position from others, like Descartes, who believed that one's existence is the conclusion of an inferential reasoning process. (Descartes expressed that reasoning process in the well known syllogism: I think, *therefore*, I am.) Calling the relation between existence and the existent "immediate" means that there is no mediating process through which the alleged predicate "existence" is joined to a subject "I". Even more, it is to claim that no such process is needed for, if the statement "I exist" (or "the world exists") refers to an "indissoluble unity" between existence and the existent, then, the statement "I exist" (or "the world exists") is an "existential indubitable" *[I, 88, 91]* Marcel argues. (What exactly he means by an *existential* rather than a logical, or rational, indubitable will become clear in a moment.)

Before moving on, however, I want to comment briefly on Marcel's arguments for the "indissoluble unity" of existence and the existent. No doubt, it is true that we can not *really* separate an existent and its existence into two separate entities. By using secondary reflection which recaptures our basic experience of the *unity* of an existent and its

---

8   MJ, 321.

9   MJ, 322.

existence, we overcome primary reflection's separation of objects from
their existence. Nevertheless, the fact that things come into and go out
of existence would seem to mean that their existence is not *indissolubly*
united to them. It is also true that nothing is more fundamental in our
lived experience than the existence of our selves and the world and that
means, as Marcel holds, that there is no more basic datum from which I
could infer my existence or the world's or could even doubt their existence.
From a phenomenological perspective, I agree that my existence (and
the world's) is "indubitable." However, to say that my existence (or the
world's existence) is experientially indubitable does not, as far as I can
see, require me to say that my existence is *indissolubly* joined to me nor
that the existence of the world is *indissolubly* joined to it. Again, such a
conclusion seems to fly in the face of the fact that I and every thing in
the world has come into existence and will cease to exist.

Be that as it may, let us move on to consider what Marcel means by
calling the self's existence an "existential" indubitable. The key is his
statement that the self's "immediate certitude" of its existence is *sensible*
in character *[I, 90]*. I find it impossible to doubt my own existence, he
claims, not because it is illogical to do so (although it is), but because I
experience a kind of "exclamatory awareness of [my] existence" *[I, 91]*,
as, for example, is manifested by a young child who shouts, leaps, and
dances in sheer delight to be alive. To say that I exist is to say, "I am
manifest," he explains, meaning "I have something to make myself known
and recognized by others and by myself" *[I, 91]* and that "something,"
of course, is "my body insofar as it is *my* body" *[I, 92]*. In other words,
for Marcel my own existence is existentially indubitable because I am
bodily and, therefore, sensibly manifest to myself and others. My bodily
existence is also the "datum on which everything else hinges" *[I, 91]*; it
is the touchstone or central reference point (*repère*) of existence he has
been seeking in this chapter, for were I to deny its existence I could not
assert the existence of anything else. Elsewhere he makes it clear that
the "everything else" he refers to in the above quotation is the existence
of other things. My body, he writes, is "the datum relative to which there
are other existents."[10] Even more striking are the following statements:
"The world *exists* in the measure in which I have relations with it which
are of the same type as my relations with my own body."[11] The existence

---

10   CF, 17.

11   MJ, 269.

of things, "is apprehended by incarnate beings like you and me, and by virtue of our being incarnate"[12] for the "sense presence" of things is the "immediate manifestation and revelation" of their existence.[13]

Marcel next reflects upon the relation between me and my body. Primary reflection, he points out, breaks the link between me and my body by taking an objective attitude toward it, an attitude that is not interested in the fact that my particular body is the only body which I experience as uniquely mine. Primary reflection considers my body as simply one body among many others, as a body which possesses essentially the same properties as all other human bodies. That, he says, is the procedure of scientific knowledge (such as anatomy or physiology) which studies my body, not in its unique relation to me, but as a human body like any other and so separates me (or my soul) and my body into two distinct things [I, 92]. For its part, secondary reflection does not claim that primary reflection is totally incorrect for it is true that my body shares features common to all human bodies. However, secondary reflection refuses to treat the separation between my self and my body as the last word because it returns to the datum prior to the activity of primary reflection, namely, to the existential indubitable which is "my body felt as *my* body" [I, 93]. Marcel emphasizes that point. Secondary reflection is not just a reflection on the results of primary reflection, for that would make it a captive of the distinctions made by primary reflection. Rather, secondary reflection calls into question the ultimate validity of primary reflection's separation of the self and its body into distinct things. It seeks to recapture their unity by returning to a fundamental level of experience, a datum more basic than the distinctions of primary reflection, where I experience my body as "intimately mine" [I, 93] and feel an "intimate connection" to it [I, 94]. Remember, we are proceeding as phenomenologists, Marcel says, "this is to say we are accepting our everyday experience." At this point it would have been helpful if he had offered descriptions of some of those everyday experiences which reveal the unity of my self with my body but, since he does not, let me offer a couple examples of my own. When a rock smashes my toe, the pain is not located in some object separate from me; I feel it *in me*. I feel the pain at and in my toe, which means that I feel my toe to be part of me.

---

12 EBHD, 47.

13 MJ, 320. No wonder he calls his epistemological position "existential realism," EBHD, 47.

Similarly, when *I* see a beautiful sunset, that seeing is not taking place in some detection device separate from me, but *in me*. My eyes seeing that sunset are *me myself* seeing that sunset. That is my experience and it is such basic everyday experiences that secondary reflection returns to in trying to understand the relation between me and my body.

Let me add that I believe Marcel was referring to such experiences at the end of his second chapter *[I, 38]* when he stated that reflection must "acknowledge that it inevitably bases itself on something which is not itself" which, he said, was an "intuition given in advance of supra-reflective unity" and is "at the root of the criticism [secondary] reflection is able to exert on itself," that is, on primary reflection. In other words, it is my basic unreflective experiences (called here intuition) of my oneness or unity with my body, experiences such as those I just described, which secondary reflection returns to and uses to critique the separation between me and my body posited by primary reflection. (In passing, Marcel also uses secondary reflection to reject the position of psycho-physical parallelism *[I, 94]* which considers the body and soul, or mind, to be two separate things which never causally interact. Even though psycho-physical parallelism admits that what goes on in the soul parallels or mirrors what goes on in the body, that position is obviously contrary to my pre-reflective feeling of my unity with my body.) Secondary reflection is able to return to the aforementioned "supra-reflective unity" (or unity prior to reflection) only because I maintain a nonreflective awareness, or intuition, of my oneness with my body. And my intuition of being my body is at the same time my immediate experience of my existence which is the existential indubitable and the central reference point for all other existents.

In order to become clearer about the intimate relation between me and my body, Marcel proceeds to discuss the notions of ownership and possession *[I, 95]*. I consider something to belong to me as my possession when there is a positive relation between us and when I take some responsibility for it and exercise some control over it. Those conditions do apply to the relation between me and my body. I feel it belongs to me, that it is my responsibility to provide for it, and to some extent that I can control it. However, he argues, something that is my possession, such as my car, is in the last analysis external to and distinct from the spatial temporal being that is me. Literally, "it does not form part of that being" *[I, 97]* and so it can be lost or stolen and I still remain myself *[I, 98]*, but that does not appear to be the case with my body. It is not independent of my being; it can't be lost or stolen like a possession can and I still remain my self. In fact, Marcel states, I can not conceive what I shall or even can be "once the link between my self and my body is broken by what I call death" *[I, 99]*. Furthermore, of what could my body be the possession? The self that owns physical things cannot be a purely nonmaterial entity (like a soul or mind) for how could a spiritual thing have any claim or care to possess physical things *[I, 97]*? Actually, my possessions, such as my car and house, are really additions to and completions *of my body*, not of a spiritual soul or mind for they protect or enhance my body's life and powers. I may even try to remove the gap between my self and my possessions so that I fuse with them and thus possess them always, but, of course, this is ultimately impossible precisely because, unlike my body, my possessions never are and cannot become identical with my very being *[I, 98]*.

If my body is not something I possess, I may be tempted to view it as an instrument through which I act on the world. But what does being an instrument imply, Marcel asks? In general an instrument is a means of reinforcing or extending the powers of a body. Accordingly, if our body itself is considered an instrument, it will have to be an instrument of another body, and that body in turn an instrument of another body, ad infinitum. We can avoid that regress by simply asserting that my body is "not an instrument at all ... [but] is in a certain sense a way of speaking of myself" *[I, 100]*. Once again, by using secondary reflection to return to the unity experienced beneath the separations of primary reflection, I "negate," "deny," "erase" any gap between me and my body. "My body is mine insofar as for me my body is not an object, but rather, I *am* my body," he affirms *[I, 100]*, which means that, "we have to bring in the idea of the body not as an object but as a subject" *[I, 101]*. In other words, my body is united with the self I am and so "I can properly assert that I am identical with my body." He hastens to add that to say I am my body must not be construed as reductive materialism, for, as we saw above, I am not just my body because it continually changes. I am also the noncontingent permanent self or subject which remains me throughout all those changes *[I, 51, 87]*.

To say I am my body, then, is an attempt to be true to my basic experience of my body as mine, or, better, as me. That experience, Marcel states, is one of feeling, "My body in so far as it is mine, presents itself to me in the first place as something felt; I am my body only in so far as I am a feeling being" *[I, 101].*[14] (From his *Metaphysical Journal*, it is clear that the kind of feelings he has in mind are those involved in internal perception, coenesthesia, as when I feel my self-body to be in pain, hungry, tired, energetic.)[15] Furthermore, my body felt as me, he says, has an "absolute priority" to everything that I can feel or sense[16] that is other than my body. That is to say, since, even before I reflect on my experience, I am nonreflectively aware, through my feelings, that I am my body, at the same time I am nonreflectively aware that my body sensing things is me sensing things. Since the "sense presence" of things is the "immediate manifestation" of their existence,[17] it follows that I am aware that I apprehend the existence of things only because I am first nonreflectively conscious that I am incarnate—-that is the reason he claims that my body, felt as me, has "absolute priority" over everything I sense that is other than my body. Of course, to put such stress on feeling or sensation naturally raises the question of their nature since some claim that we never sense or feel anything other than our own body and its modifications *[I, 102].* In his next lecture, then, Marcel will investigate the nature of feeling/sensing.

Before moving on I want to mention briefly that since in this fifth lecture he has linked his notion of existence to the sense presence of my self and things, spiritual entities (such as ideas, God, one's noncontingent self) cannot strictly speaking be said to exist. Of course, they can still "be" or be "real" or "actual." Marcel's limitation of existence to that which can be sensed or felt will cause difficulties for him, as we shall see when we get into Volume II.

Pages in other works that treat material of this chapter:
CF, 15-23, 65-66, 101-02, 108-113.   MJ, 319-27, 332-38.
EBHD, 45-47.   TW, 15, 220-22.   BH, 154-163.

---

14 My translation from ME, I, 117.

15 MJ, 243.

16 The French word is *sentir* which can be translated both as feel and as sense.

17 MJ, 320.

6

FEELING AS A MODE OF PARTICIPATION

I will begin my commentary by saying something about the term "feeling" which appears in Marcel's title and throughout the chapter. The French word is *sentir* which is normally a verb although he often uses it as a noun, *le sentir*. Like the English word feeling, *sentir* has a variety of meanings in French. In this chapter it most often means to sense or perceive something other than my body by using my senses of sight, hearing, touch, taste and smell. Sometimes *sentir* is used interchangeably with *sensation*, a French word that also can be translated as sensation or feeling. Only infrequently does Marcel use *sentir* as he did in the last chapter to refer to my *internal* feelings of my body. In order to reflect the twofold meaning of *sentir*, I will occasionally, when the context seems to require it, write the two words together, thus, sensing/feeling.

Marcel begins this lecture with a brief review of some of the ground covered in his previous one. He recalls that his point of departure in Chapter 5 was the question, "Who am I?" which became the question, what connection does my being, "my way of existence," have with my body? *[I, 103]*. As we saw, he argued that my body should not be conceived as a possession or instrument external to me but as something I *am*, which, however, must not be interpreted materialistically. Yet, he now admits, it is necessary at times to treat my body as if it were a detached object like any other human body. In order for me to communicate with my physical therapist or surgeon, I have to consider my body as they do, namely as an object, (even though it is really impossible to detach it from myself). That is the point of his reference here to truth and the intelligible milieu of Chapter 4 *[I, 104]*. In order to communicate with each other, people must be together in a common truth seeking milieu and that means they must adopt much the same way of looking at things, which in this case means viewing my body as an object. However, insofar as the body is mine, and no other body is mine in such an intimate way, we must, as he said at the end of the last chapter, emphasize the notion of feeling, for my body is the only one whose fatigue or liveliness or pain I feel. That raises the difficult questions, "What, after all, *is* feeling [*sentir*] and how is feeling [*sentir*] possible?" which, he says, is to "ask about sensation [*sensation*] in general and ask ourselves how it is possible" [*I*, 105].[1]

If we approach sensation from the perspective of primary reflection, Marcel points out, we cannot help thinking of it objectively as stimuli or messages sent out by some object (light rays coming from the pale blue sky or sound waves coming from a harp, for example) that travel through space and are received by a subject conceived as a physical reception apparatus which then transcribes or translates them into visual experiences of pale blue or auditory experiences of harp music [*I, 105*]. (What color or sound or any other sensible feature is in and for the object from which it emanates is, he observes, beyond the scope of the phenomenological method which is confined to that which is experienced by ourselves as conscious organisms.)[2] The question is, whether the notion of sensation as transcription or translation of messages emitted from an object makes any sense [*I, 106*].

Now translation, he points out, involves the replacement of one set of data (for example, English words) for another set of data (French words) according to some code (a French-English dictionary). That requires *both* sets of data (the French and the English words) to be "fully accessible to the mind" [*I, 107*] in order for translation from one to the other to occur. Yet, nothing like that can take place in the case of sensation. The original physical stimuli emitted from some object are not data I can actually sense, since in the theory in question sensation involves translation and the original stimuli, as data which are to be translated into sensations, are themselves, therefore, prior to translation. The stimuli are just "physical events" which modify our outer and inner organs but they are not, and cannot be, actually sensed by us since they themselves are not the result of translation. Some try to claim that the stimuli are "unsensed sensa," that is, like sensations but not actually sensed [*I, 107-08*] but, Marcel responds, what can unsensed sensa mean, for if they are unsensed then by definition we do not sense them and so, once again, we can not translate them into sensible colors, sounds, odors, or any other sensible quality. (May I add that in fact all the stimuli that are transmitted by external objects and received by my sense organs become

---

1   My translation from ME, I, 120-21.

2   Marcel refers to the panpsychist hypothesis that in some minimal way even an apparently nonsentient object like a flower is conscious of its sensible features such as its color or odor, *I, 105-06*.

electrical impulses in my body which travel along pathways from those organs to my spinal cord and brain and those electrical stimuli never themselves at any time possess the sensible features, the color or sound or odor, that I actually see or hear or smell.) Furthermore, he notes, if one adopts the transmission/translation explanation of sensation, solipsism becomes a serious temptation for I, as the terminus which receives and translates stimuli, could be aware only of the translated data *within* me or my brain and not the real things in the world which emit the stimuli *[I, 110]*.

Fortunately, secondary reflection comes to the rescue by recognizing that the basic assumptions of primary reflection, namely that sensation is the transmission, reception and translation of messages, must be called into question. For one thing, "every kind of message ... *presupposes* the existence of sensation" *[I, 108]*, he argues, for in order to translate a message we must first sense that message; therefore, sensation itself cannot be translation. That says what sensation is not. Can we give a positive account of it, Marcel asks, and reminds us that the entire discussion of the body and sensation/feeling in the previous chapter began with the question, "Who am I?".

In addressing that question in Chapter 5, Marcel stated that the assertion "I exist" expressed a "pure immediacy," an "indissoluble unity" *[I, 90]*, between I and exist. That meant, he explained, that I exist was not a conclusion reached by mediation for to mediate means to pass through intermediary steps in order to reach a terminus *[I, 108]*. However, there is no mediating process, such as reasoning, through which an alleged predicate (exists) is joined to a subject (I), nor is one needed. Speaking as a phenomenologist, he argued that nothing is more fundamental in my experience than my existence (and the world's) which means that there is no more basic data from which I could reason to my (or the world's) existence. My existence is, therefore, an "existential indubitable" *[I, 88, 91]*, he asserted, and my "immediate certitude" of my existence was joined to my feeling my body as mine *[I, 90]*. Now in Chapter 6, after rejecting the transmission/translation explanation of sensation, Marcel refers again to my body and to "the feeling [*sentir*] which is not separable from my body as mine" and says it is "a *non-mediatizable immediate* which is the very root of our existence" and the touchstone or reference point "of existence in general" *[I, 109]*. The "existential immediate that ... I *am*," namely, my felt bodily self, is non-mediatizable, he explains here, because it "cannot be treated as a thought-content" *[I,*

111], although it can be thought about, as we have been doing. Rather it "transcends any thought-content which can be inserted into it," he claims.

One reason he gives for saying that my existence cannot be treated as a content of thought, that is, as a concept or idea, is that every content of thought "gives rise to mediations and is a thought-content only through mediations" *[I, 111]*. I believe what he means is that every concept, (for example, of a house), inevitably gives rise to or implies other concepts (for example, concepts of walls, roof, foundation, and so on) and is known only by reference to (that is, mediated by) those other concepts. To claim, then, that my felt embodied self, "the existential immediate that ... I am," is not a "thought-content" means not only that it is not a conclusion reached by a thought process but also that it is not known by means of other concepts of thought. Rather, the most fundamental datum of my existence, my body as me, is at bottom not a thought or concept at all but a *felt* experience for Marcel, an experience which is the underlying basis of all my activity of thought—even though it "transcends every thought content ... inserted into it."

To say that my felt bodily existence "transcends any thought-content ... inserted into it" means, I think, that there is always much more in my lived experience than can be fully and adequately grasped by thought and expressed in language. The richness and depth of my "exclamatory awareness of [my] existence," the welter of feelings expressed as "Oh," "Ugh," "Alas," "Ah me" *[I, 111]* simply cannot be captured or articulated by thought. Again, that is because my experience of my existence is not a concept or idea of thought, nor a conclusion arrived at by thought, but an immediate lived experience of *feeling*, my feeling embodied.

Although Marcel does repeat here that my certitude that I exist is the touchstone or reference point of "existence in general" *[I, 109]*, he does not go on in *The Mystery*... to explicitly connect my awareness of the existence of other things with sensation. Since he did so in his earlier *Metaphysical Journal*, let us turn again to it. The first thing to note is that in that work he says many of the same things about sensation that he does here in *The Mystery* ... about my bodily existence. For instance, in the *Metaphysical Journal* he states that, like our experience of our bodily existence, sensation is a *"pure* immediate ... which by its very essence is incapable of mediation."[3] There are no mental steps one can go through, such as translation or reasoning, to derive or construct

3   MJ, 329. See also, 331.

sensation, for sensation is our most fundamental experience. In fact, feeling embodied and sensing the world are "data *on which the mind must be based*"[4] to perform any activity, he says, including those of translation and reasoning. In other words, for Marcel, just as my body's internal senses *immediately* reveal my own bodily existence, so also my body's external senses *immediately* reveal the existence of things in the world. Passages that I cited in the previous chapter make this clear. "The world *exists* in the measure in which I have relations with it which are of the same type," namely, sensory, "as my relations with my own body."[5] The existence of things "is apprehended by incarnate beings like you and me, and by virtue of our being incarnate,"[6] for the "sense presence" of things is the "*immediate* manifestation and revelation" of their existence.[7]

Because sensation is immediate, the best way to think of it, Marcel suggests, is as participation and he devotes the rest of this chapter to a discussion of that topic. There are different kinds of participation, he explains *[I, 111-14]*. At one end of the scale, people can share or participate in some objective reality like a cake—each one takes a part of it. At the other end, people can participate with others in some ceremony or action where there is almost no external object at all. He gives as an example of the second kind of participation, a multitude of people praying to God who are "melted into a single love." He calls that participation "nonobjective participation" and goes on to say that non-objectivity is "the condition of the reality of participation itself" *[I, 113]*. His choice of the term "melted" to designate nonobjective participation makes that clear for it expresses not an objective relation of subjects to an external object, but rather a *union* of subjects participating in and with each other.

Marcel next distinguishes two kinds of nonobjective participation, emergent and submerged *[I, 113-14]*. The former refers to participation that "emerges" around a conscious idea, such as God, a war, a goal. The latter is called submerged since it is beneath the threshold of conscious thought and will, although it can be reflected upon and illuminated by thought and thus emerge to some degree. Sensation/feeling, he says, is

4   MJ, 338. See also 331.

5   MJ, 269.

6   EBHD, 47.

7   MJ, 320; I have added the emphasis. Note that insofar as sensation is an immediate awareness of existing things, it too can be called an intuition.

participation at a submerged level *[I, 114]* meaning, apparently, that I
sense and feel myself and other things most of the time without explicitly
reflecting on the fact I am doing so, without deliberately willing to do
so, and without knowing exactly how I do so. Of course, in this chapter
he is deliberately directing his conscious reflection on the participation
present in sensing/feeling; he is using secondary reflection to reach the
unity beneath the separations posited by primary reflection and also
to overcome misleading physical images of submerged participation *[I,
114]*.

What really matters for participation, he asserts, is "a certain interior
disposition,"[8] such as a strong desire to join with others in a common
task, such as defense of the oppressed. But that conscious will to participate with others in a common effort is only possible, he claims, "on the
basis of a kind of consensus ... literally merely a common *feeling* about
something" *[I, 115]*, such as the injustice of oppression. That common
feeling, as "something felt rather than something thought," is an instance
of submerged participation among people and it is because that feeling
is shared that I and others who share it can subsequently consciously
and deliberately will to join together in common actions to liberate the
oppressed. That is, we can unite in forms of emergent participation
because of the submerged participation we already share.

We have been speaking of participation between persons but there
is, Marcel proposes, a vast reality of participation which goes beyond
interpersonal relations, such as the links or bonds between a peasant and
the soil, the sailor and the sea, a person and his or her neighborhood.
If we look more deeply into the nature of such bonds, he suggests, we
may be better able to understand participation and the specific nature
of the participation present in sensing/feeling *[I, 115-16]*. (However,
while his discussion does go deeper into the notion of participation in
general, he does not in fact say a great deal about the specific character
of sensory participation.) As we have seen, to speak of nonobjective
participation is, negatively, to deny that the relation between participants and that in which they participate is external. Positively, it is to
emphasize the links, bonds, and union between the participants and
that in which they participate. Accordingly, Marcel states that the
participatory relation between the peasant and the land to which he is
emotionally attached is a bond such that the soil is "linked to his inner

---

8   My translation from ME, I, 131.

being" and is experienced "as a sort of inner presence"[9] [I, 116], that is, as an intimate part of his inner life. The peasant's relation to the soil does not just affect him externally, like, for example, a dust storm that can choke and blind him; rather his bond with it means that the soil also affects him internally, that is, it affects his thoughts, feelings, and choices.

Since Marcel does not provide any illustrations of that bond, I will offer my own. We who live almost entirely in a man made technological environment might better understand the participation of the peasant and the soil if we contrast our mechanically ordered life, largely divorced from any direct contact with nature, with that of the farmer. The latter's life is tied to the alterations and rhythms of nature, the changes of the weather, the cycles of the seasons; the farmer must patiently learn to adapt to the variable but regular climate of his region. He or she must understand and willingly cooperate with the intrinsic laws of growth of different living things as they develop to maturity, nourishing and caring for them by responding to their inner needs. The farmer cannot force living things to conform to a totally artificial clock regulated pace of life if he or she hopes to enhance their growth. Similarly, he or she must understand and submit to the needs of the soil itself if it is to remain fertile. Furthermore, because of his or her ties to nature, the farmer is far more likely to acknowledge the human being's utter dependence on it and to appreciate its awesome power and beauty—both beyond human control. On the other hand, individuals who live mostly in an environment of technologically transformed nature may succumb to the temptation to view themselves as separate from nature and as lords and masters of it and so consider natural things simply as objects or raw material to be dominated and manipulated and turned into useful products.

Now just as the participation of the farmer with nature is a form of nonobjective submerged participation, so too, as he said, is sensation/feeling for Marcel. Especially in the previous chapter, we saw that he considers my internal sensing or feeling of my body to be immediate and indubitable evidence of my oneness with (participation in) my body and, therefore, of my existence. Likewise, he claimed that the existence of the world is immediate and indubitable for me because my sensing of the world is an immediate nonobjective participation or union with other physical things. In other words, the indubitability of both my

9   He will discuss his notion of presence in Chapter 10.

and the world's existence is grounded in the participation, the union with them, that I experience in sensation and feeling. To cite again a passage from his *Metaphysical Journal*, "between me and all that exists there is a relation ... of the same type as the relation that unites me to my body,"[10] and that relation is one of submerged nonobjective participation revealed in my sensing or feeling. Accordingly, just as Marcel speaks of my oneness with my body, so also he refers to my union with the things I sense: "to experience a sensation is really to become in some manner the thing sensed ... a sort of temporary coalescence is established" between us.[11] Again, "sensation ... must involve the immediate participation of what we normally call the subject in a surrounding world from which no real frontier separates it."[12] Borrowing a phrase from Heidegger, he writes, "sensation is in reality a mode of *being in the world*"[13] for through sensation "I am really *attached* to and really adhere to all that exists—to the universe which is my universe and whose center is my body."[14] The following statement at the end of his *Metaphysical Journal* offers a succinct summation of his position by joining together sensation, participation, my body, and existence. "Sensation (= the fact of sensing, of participating in a universe which creates me by affecting me) and the intellectually indefectible bond which unites me with what I call my body ... these are merged together at the heart of existence."[15]

Returning to his discussion of participation in *The Mystery of Being*, Marcel explains that nonobjective participation must be understood as transcending "the traditional opposition between activity and passivity" [I, 117] for "effective participation," he says, involves *both* features. For example, the active will to participate with others in a common task is accompanied by a passive feeling that one is being carried along and supported by a shared energy [I, 117, 113]. As for sensation and feeling, they clearly have a receptive side for one is affected by the sensible features of things and the internal states of one's body, and most of

10   MJ, 274.

11   MJ, 257.

12   MJ, 331-32. I have slightly modified the English translation of *Journal métaphysique* (Paris: Gallimard, 1927), 322.

13   EBHD, 45.

14   MJ, 274.

15   MJ, 338. I have slightly modified the English translation of *Journal métaphysique*, 328.

these affects are submerged beneath, or at least prior to, any deliberate conscious effort to sense or feel. However, sensation and feeling also have an active side. To explain, he proposes an analogy with the kind of receiving involved when I welcome guests into my house or some other environment that I have actively impregnated with certain features of myself—such as by decorating or arranging it in preparation for them.[16] Such receptivity *actively* makes room in that environment for the other person. I receive (passive) my guests and invite them (active) to partici- pate with me in this personal region I have prepared *[I, 118]*. Applying this to sensation, it is an activity insofar as it involves opening myself to receive (the passive side) the thing sensed. Indeed, I can decide on the extent to which I am open for I can choose which sensible features and things I will pay attention to and how receptive I will be to them. Often, I miss some of the physical beauty of things because I am too preoccupied to notice or be actively responsive to them.

Of course, my body is central in all this for when I sense something I actively receive it, not just into a region impregnated with myself, but into my very being, my embodied self. Let us repeat, however, that does not mean that Marcel believes that sensation takes place *within* one's body; to think that would be again to use primary reflection to separate the sensing subject from the sensed object. In secondary reflection we become aware of our fundamental prereflective experience of sensation as a union or participation with the sensed thing. We recognize that when we sense a tree, it is indeed the tree itself that we see, touch and hear, not some message transmitted by light or sound waves from an object to our brains. Again, for Marcel, to sense something is to "become in some manner the thing sensed;"[17] that is, it is to allow a physical be- ing to participate in our embodied being and also to extend ourselves to participate in its reality. That is true, he says, for all beings who are sentient, even those minimally so (worms, slugs). To sense is for them to be in union with what they sense so that they and the sensed existent participate, however minimally, in each other's being *[I, 119]*.

The final pages of Chapter 6 are devoted to a discussion of the dif- ference between a participatory and a nonparticipatory approach to natural things *[I, 120-24]*. To explain the difference, Marcel distin- guishes between the responses of a scientific technician and of an artist to a flower. The former, whom he describes as interested in mastering

16 See also CF, 28-29.

17 MJ, 257.

nature, desires to create in the laboratory a set of conditions which will produce a living flower. The artist, on the other hand, simply wants to "recreate" the fully developed flower in a painting or sculpture. The technological approach, which desires to produce living things (and which, he states, must be considered sacrilegious from a religious point of view), refuses to participate in the reality of the flower *[I, 120]*. The artist's intention to recreate the flower, on the other hand, is possible only through participation. The artist appreciates the beautiful reality of the flower as it is and seeks to enter into its very being in order to recreate it in a work of art *[I, 123]*.

That discussion reminds Marcel of the distinction he made in an earlier work, *Being and Having*, between "man as spectator and man as a participator" *[I, 121]*. There he described the spectator as an uncommitted, somewhat curious, observer of things, not personally involved in the scene he or she observes. The participator, of course, is personally involved since he or she is united to the reality in question. Now, he adds, he wants to introduce a third alternative, namely, the case of the contemplative. Contemplation, he claims, unlike curiosity which is oriented toward the future, is interested only in a present reality and is a most intimate mode of participation in that reality, a deep "grip on the real" *[I, 123]*. Contemplative participation is present in every true artist, he states, and is, of course, the opposite of a spectator's detached attitude. The case of the technician, he admits, is more complicated since he or she is not a mere spectator yet also not a "properly creative spirit" [I, 124] like the artist, apparently because the technician desires to master and manipulate, not to participate in, the reality of things. He concludes this chapter without any further discussion of these distinctions, although he does begin his next lecture by returning briefly to the topic of contemplation.

Pages in other works that treat material in this chapter:
CF, 24-29, 88-92.   EBHD, Chapter 3.
MJ, 256-60, 268-69, 274-78, 327-32, 338. TW, 48-51.

7

BEING IN A SITUATION

The seventh lecture begins with Marcel recalling some of the items of the sixth. He repeats that sensation/feeling must be understood as modes of participation but adds that the notion of participation is wider than sensation. There are higher senses of participation, he states, one of which, contemplation, was mentioned at the end of the last lecture and we need to emphasize such higher forms in order to obtain a clearer response to the overriding question we have been asking: Who or what am I? [I, 125]. This lecture will in fact directly address and offer some response to that question. Let me note, however, Marcel admits at the beginning of the next chapter, that in this seventh chapter he wanders around quite a bit and is "tempted into several side paths" [I, 148]. Because of this, my exposition will also have to jump around in his text so that I can group together and explain the scattered statements he makes on particular topics.

An analysis of various kinds of looking will help us better understand contemplation, Marcel says. One form may be totally in the service of some practical activity, such as a person looking for a path to a specific destination. Another kind of looking, whose goal is not practical in the same sense since it seeks only knowledge, is that undertaken by a scientist who looks for a specimen of a particular species of plant, mineral or animal. The looking involved in contemplation, however, is neither practical nor for a specimen of a class, but for a *unique* object —if, indeed it even has an object in the ordinary sense, that is, something external to the contemplating self. When looking becomes contemplation, he explains, it can turn its direction inwards, as when we use the term contemplation to refer to the act by which "the self concentrates its attention on itself" [I, 126].[1] Contemplation of one's self is a turning inwards of one's awareness of the world. It involves, he says, an inward gathering together or collecting of one's thoughts, which he calls recollection,[2] in

---

1   My translation from ME, I, 142.

2   Throughout Volume I, the English translator renders the French word *recueillment* as "ingatheredness;" however, that is not an English word. To my knowledge, all other translations in all of Marcel's other works (including

the presence of whatever worldly situation is being contemplated in such a way that the worldly reality enters into the recollection *[I, 126].* In other words, recollection is an act of turning inwards without leaving out the contemplated worldly reality *[I, 129].* All this is extremely abstract but fortunately, as a good phenomenologist, Marcel furnishes an illuminating example from a classical French tragedy, *Cinna,* which contains all the elements of recollection: turning inwards or reflecting on one's self, gathering together of one's thoughts, and the worldly reality or situation which enters into the recollection.

In the play, the Emperor Augustus discovers that some of those on whom he has lavished favors are leading a plot on his life. Controlling his immediate angry reaction to that discovery, he turns inward to look at himself and his perilous situation. In turning over the treachery in his mind, he tries to view it from the perspective of the conspirators who truly believe that by killing him they are ridding Rome of tyranny. Eventually in his recollection, Augustus comes to the realization that he himself is responsible for his situation, since in the past he has acted in the very same way as his conspirators, for he has spilt much blood including that of his friends and his tutor *[I, 130-31].* As a result, he is forced to ask himself whether he has any right to condemn those who seek to kill him.

In the example it is obvious that Augustus' predicament is not a mere objective spectacle for him and that he is not a detached spectator of it *[I, 126-28].* His friends' treachery, which he turns over in his mind and which prompts his reflection into his deeper self, is not external to him but joined to his very being. Does that mean it is within or inside of him, Marcel asks, and responds that in contemplation and recollection the spatial oppositions between outside and inside, inner and outer, generated by primary reflection, are transcended *[I, 128].* That is, the reality I am contemplating is not within me as if I were a container like a box with things inside of it; nor is it outside of me as if I am an hermetically sealed being isolated from the realities of the world. Rather, he says, I am truly bound, linked in my very being, to those realities

---

Volume II of this work) translate *recueillment* as recollection, and so will I. The French term can also be translated as contemplation. The verb *recueillir* means to gather or collect; *se recueillir* is also to gather or collect, as, for example, one's thoughts. Marcel uses all those forms here.

I contemplate, "a certain *coesse*" (oneness of being) is realized between them and me *[I, 128].*[3]

Another thing that the example shows clearly is the different meanings or levels of the self. (This is not a new point. Marcel referred to various levels of the self in Chapter 4 when he spoke of one part of the self seeking truth and another part refusing to face it.) He distinguishes within Augustus the self of reflection and recollection from the self of lust and vengeance—at the same time insisting that they are not two separable selves but "different modulations ... of one and the same subject" *[I, 130].* Augustus, he says, is someone who enters into the depths of himself and so gets out of, or better, disengages himself from, the self that he normally is *[I, 131].* (Such disengagement, Marcel says elsewhere, shows that we are free.)[4] Recollection, then, involves one anxiously questioning him or her self about the relation between one's deeper self and one's life, the latter traditionally called one's empirical self *[I, 132].* (My empirical self, he explains in another work, "can be reduced to a whole made up of objectively definable characteristics,"[5] such as my particular feelings, thoughts, values, personality, character, particular physical features, and particular history.) In fact, recollection may well prompt a decision to change one's life or empirical self and so involve what Marcel refers to as "an act of inner creativity or transmutation" of my self *[I, 132].*

To speak about the relation between my self and my life or empirical self forces us, Marcel states, into a discussion of the relation between me and my situation, a relation he designates as "being in a situation" *[I, 132].* We cannot, he insists, treat the given determinate features that constitute our empirical selves as "contingent" in relation to some kind of abstract pure selves. To consider my empirical features as contingent would be to view them as removable from an alleged "transcendental kernel" which would be my pure and true self *[I, 133].* That kernel, which presently has certain empirical features and occupies a particular situation, could allegedly have very different features and occupy some other situation and, if it did, it would supposedly remain essentially

---

3   My translation from ME, I, 144.

4   EBHD, 95; CA, 181. On the last page of this chapter Marcel seems to have this free disengagement in mind when he speaks of a positive form of "aloofness" I, 147.

5   "An Essay..." in PE, 120.

the same kernel, that is, the same pure transcendental self.[6] On the contrary, Marcel contends, we are not autonomous, self-contained and self-sufficient beings whose essential reality is independent of the concrete circumstances in which we live. The concrete situations of our lives are not objective relations which exist independent of us for our being is totally exposed, vulnerable, and permeable to the situations in which we exist *[I, 144-46]*. Using a beautiful metaphor, he writes, "I am in the world only insofar as the world ... [is] something shaping me as in a womb"[7] and a kind of "primordial bond, a kind of umbilical cord ... unites the human being to a particular, determined and concrete environment."[8] His point is that the self that I am is to a great extent the result of the particular circumstances in which I have lived and with which I have interacted throughout my life. To illustrate: to a large degree, I am the individual self I am because I was born and raised by two loving parents in the United States, rather than by a single parent in India, learned English rather that Hindi, was raised in a middle class home that fostered education rather than in one whose poverty made education impossible, was raised Catholic rather than Hindu, and so on. It is a "fiction," Marcel stresses, to think that what I am could be understood by attempting to abstract or separate my self from the concrete circumstances in which I have lived and that means that my empirical self and the empirical circumstances of my life are "noncontingent" in relation to me *[I, 133-34]*. Elsewhere he puts it this way, the "fundamental situation which is mine ... shapes me into myself"[9] and the particular circumstances of my life are "in the strict sense of the term *constitutive*" *[I, 134]* of my self for I am bound to them in a relation of participation.[10]

Still, there is more that must be said for it is not the case that the circumstances in which I live *unilaterally* constitute me. To speak of my relation to them as one of participation means that they are joined to me and that in turn means that the given circumstances of my life do not have "a real, embodied, independent existence *outside* the self" *[I, 134]* and have no "autonomous validity" or "authority" in themselves *[I,*

6   CF, 22, 83.

7   CF, 29.

8   TW, 38.

9   EBHD, 83.

10   CF, 29, 70.

135]. Rather, the factors in our situation "come into our lives" and take on "reverberatory power," that is, have meaning for us and affect us, only through a "free activity" on our part *[I, 134-35]* and thus one's situation is not something one just "passively suffers, but actively lives" *[I, 144].* Insofar as I am aware of the circumstances in which I live and choose to interact with them in particular ways, they affect me, not just externally, but in the "inward" dimension of my life, my thoughts, feelings, values, choices, and so forth. In other words, it is my *active* participation in my situation which forms my very being. A concrete example might be helpful. Suppose a person grows up in an isolated neighborhood which has no children his or her age. That situation could influence the individual in various ways. It could encourage a love of books and a reserve around people. It could prompt the individual to become fearful of others and even downright antisocial. It could provoke the individual to aggressively search for friends. The point is the kind of individual the person becomes is not simply the effect of the childhood circumstance of living in an isolated neighborhood but is due to the way he or she chose to interact with, and participate in, that situation. Perhaps the best way to put it would be to say that in and through our inward interaction with our situation, we have shaped and created ourselves into particular kinds of persons *[I, 138-39].* The paths we have chosen have made all the difference. Such a "creative interchange" with my situation involves, Marcel reminds us, the active side of receptivity discussed earlier *[I, 145].*[11]

Before concluding my commentary on Marcel's discussion of the noncontingency of my situation and my empirical self, we ought to recall that in Chapter 5 he apparently took the very opposite position, for he said there "that the definite characteristics of the self insofar as I grasp it as a particular individual [namely, as the empirical self] have a contingent [NB] character ... in relation to myself as a subject" *[I, 86-87].* Let me try to resolve his contradictory remarks. On the one hand, I am in fact a particular concrete self having certain describable features; however, those features have a contingent (non-necessary) relation to me in the following way. Many concrete situations in my life could have been different and I could have made different choices and reacted in different ways to the circumstances I faced. My parents could have moved to a different region of the country or given me up for adoption. My father could have been killed in war. If such things had

11 Marcel uses the phrase "creative interchange" on CF, 70 and 71.

happened, surely I would be different than I am now. Nevertheless, in those scenarios, I would still in some deep sense be the same singular subject, the same unique self, I now am; I would not have turned into some other self. That is to say, I would be the same unique person even if my lived history were very different.[12] On the other hand, it is also true that the particular *empirical* self I am now was created by my interchange with the particular situations I did in fact live and participate in, and in that sense those situations are "noncontingent" in relation to my present empirical self with its objectively definable characteristics. Nevertheless, to repeat, there is a deeper dimension of me, namely, the permanent self that never becomes some other self. Gabriel Marcel would never become Jean-Paul Sartre or Simone de Beauvoir even if the particular characteristics of his self and the concrete situations of his life had been radically different. And insofar as they might have been different, they can be said to be "contingent" in relation to his permanent self. To sum it up, one's particular situation and empirical characteristics are contingent in relation to his or her permanent self; they are not contingent in relation to the particular empirical self one has in fact become by interacting with the concrete situations that were actually present in one's life.

There are even more dimensions of the self for Marcel than the two just mentioned, as we shall see as we return to his discussion of recollection.[13] He quotes a passage from one of his early works, "*Positions et approches concrètes du mystère ontologique,*"[14] in which he states that in recollection's turning within one's self, one becomes able to evaluate his or her life [*I, 136*]. As we saw earlier, when I turn within myself in recollection, I detach myself from the actual life I have been living, yet that life is still included in my reflection on myself. That means that recollection enables us "to become aware of a gap between our beings

---

12   In Chapter 9, Marcel will directly address the question, what constitutes one's permanent identity throughout his/her life?

13   Later in this chapter, *I, 140-44,* Marcel examines the notion of reconnoitering, which he describes as an attempt to find our way in ourselves by trying to recognize what we live for, that is, what is of real interest and importance to us. Since, as far as I can see, to reconnoiter within ourselves means to recollect, and his discussion of reconnoitering adds little to his discussion of recollection, I am not going to summarize his treatment of it.

14   CA, 182. The translation I am using renders the title "Concrete Approaches to Investigating the Ontological Mystery."

and our lives" and so be able to judge our lives. In recollection, he says, "I am weighing the actual life I have been leading in the balance of the potential life I carry within me, the life that I aspire to lead, the life I would have to lead if I wanted to become fully myself" [I, 137]. Note that in those passages, Marcel identifies my "being" with the ideal life or self within me that I aspire to live and would have to live in order to come to *be* my full self.

Actually, in his essay "Concrete Approaches ...," just a little beyond the passage he cites in *The Mystery...*, Marcel adds a brief, but important, statement about my being or my ideal self that he does not include here. "The I into which I return [in recollection]," he states, "ceases ... to belong to itself."[15] However, except for mentioning St. Paul's words, "You are not your own," he does not explain what he means. Similar assertions can be found in other works. For example, in *The Existential Background of Human Dignity*, using his favorite metaphor, he states that the self to which I have to be true in order to become fully myself is a light. (Recall that in Chapter 4 truth was referred to as light.) Recollection, he says, involves establishing contact with a source of illumination, a light which can light up my life and enable me to judge it, a light that can guide me toward creating a fuller or truer self. Yet this light, he maintains, "has been bestowed on me;" it is not my own creation.[16] Similarly, in the second volume of *The Mystery of Being*, he asserts that our "being is something that can only be granted to us as a gift ... it is a crude illusion to believe that it is something I can give myself" [II, 32]. In these texts, it seems clear that Marcel is claiming that our ideal self, our being, the light which guides us, does not belong to us since it is not something we give ourselves; it is not our own creation but a gift bestowed on us.

How can he make this claim? Experience does seem to bear out his belief that we have within ourselves some, at least vague, notion of the ideal self we should become and that we do use it to judge the lives we have been living. Still, why say that ideal can not be our own or society's creation? To look ahead, Marcel's answer is suggested in his next chapter when he talks about individuals who accept great sufferings and hardships and are even willing to sacrifice their lives in order to be true to themselves, that is, in order to become the selves they should be [I, 166].

---

15   CA, 182.

16   EBHD, 88, 95.

Such persons would be foolish to take an ideal created by human will so seriously; if I produced my own ideal self, I could simply remake it more to my liking when its demands became too painful. Yet that is precisely what I feel I should not do, for I experience that ideal as the "self to which I *have to* be true" [*I, 143*, my emphasis], the self I *should* become, the self, he says in *Homo Viator*, I am "commanded" to become.[17] And if I refuse that ideal I will not find it easy to excuse myself; rather I will feel I have been unfaithful to a most serious obligation. In fact, if we deny the reality of our being or ideal self; that is, if we claim that it is simply our own creation, Marcel contends, we will be unable to evaluate our lives except by some totally arbitrary standards which we ourselves have chosen, and that amounts to "a radical scepticism" about any self-evaluation, which "is nothing more than despair."[18]

In *The Mystery...* Marcel also refers to my ideal self, the self I should become, as something which calls me as my "personal vocation" [*I, 137*]. A vocation, he explains, is experienced not as fate, that is, as something I must inevitably follow, but as an appeal, perhaps even as a "cry that comes out to me from my own depths" [*I, 143*]. Yet, like my ideal self, my vocation, is not contingent either, meaning, apparently, that it is not just my own or others' arbitrary free creation. I experience my vocation, he says, as something "which imposes itself on me" [*I, 137*] and "commands" me to sacrifice my personal self-interest.[19] In *Homo Viator* Marcel points to the vocations experienced by priests, doctors, artists and soldiers, who feel called and obligated to place themselves at the disposal of a "superior order" or "causes" greater than they, such as justice, peace, love, and beauty. Of course, people are free to ignore or to dismiss their vocations as nothing but the creations of their own superegos or of society, but to do so, he says, will not free them from experiencing the obligation to follow their calling.[20] Nor, of course, can it explain the guilt one feels for not responding to his or her voca-

---

17 HV, 106. See also, 8, 25, 105-07. He says something similar in CF, 77-78 and MB, II, 31-32.

18 CA, 182.

19 HV, 106.

20 HV, 25-26, 105-06. Recall that in Chapter 1 Marcel said he was responding to a call to give these lectures, a "demand" he felt he could not reject "without becoming guilty of ... an indefensible betrayal," I, 2. In addition, he described the philosopher as someone who hears the call to pursue truth.

tion, nor the astonishing fact that many do answer its call even at great personal risk. But if our vocation or ideal self is not a human creation, what, according to Marcel, is its source? He will suggest an answer in Volume II.

To summarize Marcel's view of recollection, it consists of reflecting deeply into my self and becoming aware of my being, my ideal self, the self I should become to be true to myself and fulfill my self. That is the same as saying that by recollection I become aware of a personal call or vocation which urges and even commands me to become fully my self. Furthermore, since I experience my ideal self or vocation to be bestowed and even imposed on me, it cannot be my own or society's creation.

Pages in other works that treat material in this chapter:
CF, 22-29, 82-92, 104-14.   HV, 23-25, 105-07, 130-32.
EBHD, 83-89, 94-95.   CA, 180-83.

8
'MY LIFE'

Marcel begins by admitting that in the previous lecture he wandered around quite a bit and so he immediately refocuses on the central question of these talks, "Who am I ... I who interrogate myself about my being?" [I, 148]. It is important to recognize that by this question he is not asking for a neutral description of his nature; rather the question is about his value: he is asking, "What am I worth?" [I, 149].

That question in turn provokes a more basic one: am I qualified to say what I am worth? After all, Marcel notes, I am not and cannot be an unbiased evaluator of my self. Perhaps, then, I should ask others, for example, a close friend or some social entity like a party, to inform me about my value. But that won't work either, for even if they can enlighten me, the truth is that I myself have selected them and decided that they are qualified; in other words, if I am not qualified to judge my worth, neither would be any others that I select. He concludes, then, that the question, "What am I worth?" is not solvable "at the human level" [I, 149].

If the question cannot be answered by human beings, we "come up against the inner demand for transcendence," Marcel says [I, 152], which in Chapter 3 he described as a demand for a purer mode of experience which would be filled with intelligibility and truth. The question, "What am I?" or "What am I worth?" becomes an appeal beyond the human realm, a "supra empirical appeal," he states, "*beyond* the limits of experience towards one who can only be described as an absolute Thou," who would be our "last and supreme resource" [I, 152]. Since he does not explain here what he means by an "absolute Thou," we must turn to other works, especially *Creative Fidelity*, for clarification. There he indicates that an absolute Thou would be a transcendent reality of "infinite plenitude"[1] and yet a person intimately related to me; that is what he means by using the familiar form of the pronoun you and referring to the transcendent as a Thou rather than a You or He or

---

1   CF, 37.

She.[2] An absolute Thou would know and love me profoundly because it would never be external to me but deep within me.[3] In other words, my relationship with such a being would be one of participation, "participation in a reality which overflows and envelopes me, without my being able to view it as in any way external to what I am."[4] Thus an absolute Thou, and only an absolute Thou, who "knows me and evaluates me"[5] from deep within myself could reveal to me what I am truly worth. Of course the crucial question, and Marcel asks it, is whether there is such "a being who hears my appeal and is capable of responding to it?"[6] In *Creative Fidelity*, as here in *The Mystery of Being*, he states that we can not "empirically" verify that there is such being since it would transcend "all possible experience."[7]

Yet, for Marcel to speak of something or someone "transcending" all experience seems to contradict what he said in Chapter 3. There he criticized philosophers for having too restrictive an idea of experience and went on to insist that the word "'transcendent' [does] not mean 'transcending experience' but on the contrary there must exist a possibility of having an experience of the transcendent as such" [I, 46]. The key to resolving his apparently contradictory assertions is, I believe, in his use of the term "supra-empirical" in *The Mystery of Being* passage given above along with a statement in *Creative Fidelity* that we cannot verify "empirically" that there is an absolute Thou for such a being would not be an "objective datum."[8] An absolute being would, of course, transcend the limits of *empirical* experience, that is, experience through the senses unaided or expanded by instruments, the kind of experiences that empirical scientists use to verify or falsify their hypotheses. However, to say that something is not an object which can be empirically verified or that it transcends all possible empirical experience does not mean that

---

2   Marcel uses the French word *tu* here rather than *vous*. In the next chapter he will discuss in some detail the difference in the relations between an I and a thou and an I and a you or he or she.

3   BH, 124-25.

4   CF, 144. See also, BH, 124-25; HV, 152.

5   CF, 145.

6   Ibid.

7   Ibid.

8   CF, 169. Similarly in BH, 125, he says that the being to whom I appeal is not an observable fact "placed before me."

the reality in question could not be encountered in some other kind of experience. In fact, we shall see in Volume II that Marcel does believe that human beings can and do have various kinds of experiences of an absolute Thou.

Rather than pursuing any further my relation to an absolute Thou, he turns to consider more mundane responses to his central question "Who am I?". The first proposal he considers is the view that I am "my whole life" [I, 154], for life presents itself to reflection as a sequence of events that can be told as a story. The problem in identifying my self with the story of my life, however, is that I can't report everything I have lived, I have to summarize. Even if I have kept a diary, I still don't remember a great deal of my life but only disconnected fragments. In addition, I can't help but interpret past episodes in light of all I have experienced since they occurred and so I inevitably give past events a structure and meaning they did not have at the time. The result is, Marcel concludes, I can't possibly tell the story of my past life as I actually lived it [I, 154-58] and so to claim that I am my whole life is not helpful since it means I am largely unknown even to myself.

The second proposal he considers is that my life (and hence my self) is my tangible accomplishments or works [I, 158-60]; that is, the artist is his paintings, a philosopher her writings. But which works, for they may be very uneven in quality and some may lack the artist's unique style and character? Furthermore, the *meaning* of a person's works is relative to his or her audience; some people have a deep appreciation of Van Gogh's paintings, others a superficial appreciation, others none at all. Also, every interpretation is done from within a particular historical vantage point and, of course, there is no way to know today how posterity will judge. Therefore, to identify someone with his or her works is to make who they are totally variable because totally relative to others. Perhaps the greatest objection to identifying one's life with his or her works, Marcel points out, is that most people do not create tangible works such as we mentioned. Still, since everyone has *done* certain things in their lives, might it not be better then to identify an individual's life (and self) with his or her deeds or acts [I, 160-61]?

Yet once again we can ask, which deed or acts, the habitual ones, the exceptional ones, or both? In fact, he says, isn't the most important thing how a person understands and reacts to the contradiction between his or her habitual acts and his or her exceptional acts; that attitude will tell us more about the person than any of his or her external acts. However, it is very possible that I will not be able to recall my state of mind or attitude at the time I did certain actions. Also, I can interpret my past actions in many different ways all of which will be conditioned by my present state of mind. If I am presently depressed, I will interpret my past actions in one way; if I am elated, in another.

A general difficulty with every one of these proposals, Marcel complains, is that they identify my life, and hence my self, with something in my past, but the fact is, "I am still caught up in my life, I am still committed to living" [I, 161-62] and insofar as I am living it, what is essential is not so much my past but what purpose or goal I am presently dedicating myself to. (Indeed, my past will itself be evaluated in terms of my goals—as either helping or hindering me from attaining them.) Furthermore, "an analysis of experience," he claims, shows, "that my sense of life' or my vivid awareness of being alive" is fluctuating, and "that the more definitely I am aiming at some purpose or other ["in which I am ... really participating"] the more vividly I am aware of being alive" and of "living in the fullest fashion" [I, 162]. (Here again we must keep in mind that Marcel's approach is phenomenological which means he focuses on my *experience* of feeling alive, my *experience* of vigor and energy, not on the actual biological health of my body.) Vivacity, of course, is the opposite of the condition of total indifference, where I have no interest in anything and no purpose or goal really matters to me [I, 163].

Now if I am more alive the more I concentrate on some goal, that naturally raises the question—what goals should I be centered on? Surely, not just on the continuation of my bodily existence, Marcel replies, for people who care only about the proper functioning of their bodies live "poverty-stricken" lives "shut up" in themselves and in their "private experience" [I, 163]. Self-centered individuals do not sympathetically and imaginatively share in the experiences of others and so deprive themselves of participating in all that is alive in them. Such people, Marcel says, are unavailable,[9] unable to respond to the many "calls" made upon them, calls, apparently, to open themselves and participate in the richness of realities beyond themselves. Thus, he concludes, it is essential to human life, that is, to our feeling of being alive, that life be

---

9   Marcel mentions (I, 63) the difficulties in translating into English the French terms *disponibilité* and *indisponibilité*. Rather than translating them as available and unavailable, he suggests we use handy and unhandy. However, the English translator disregards his suggestion and continues to use available and unavailable, and I will do the same.

oriented to a reality transcending itself, a reality which will give it its purpose or "point and in a certain sense even its justification" [I, 164].

These reflections prompt Marcel to think about those who are willing to give their lives for some thing, for a cause such as peace or justice, for example. How can a goal furnish justification for the hero's or martyr's life, if it calls them to sacrifice that life; after all, my life is not my possession like my car that I can give away and still remain alive. Nevertheless, Marcel asserts that I can give my life "without ceasing to be myself" for the truth is that sacrifice of one's life "is essentially creative" not destructive of one's self [I, 165]. To see that, however, we must not understand the essence of self-sacrifice rationally, by which he means as an exchange of goods where I give something in order to get something in return. Obviously, those who give their lives without any hope of surviving death cannot be doing so in order to get anything. That is why from a common sense point of view, to give up everything for nothing is utter madness [I, 165].

But rational common sense looks at self-sacrifice from the outside and Marcel advises us instead to use secondary reflection and join ourselves sympathetically with the "inner essence" of the sacrificial act. In other words, let us attempt to participate in the acts and experiences of the hero or martyr. If we do so, we will recognize, he believes, that such a person feels that if he shrank from giving his life, he would be "falling below himself" [I, 166]. In the terms used in the previous chapter, we could say that he feels he is failing to respond to his vocation to be true to the ideal self he should become. Therefore, if we sympathetically participate in the experience of the person who offers his life, we will recognize, Marcel claims, that he "has, without any doubt at all, the feeling that through self-sacrifice he is reaching self-fulfillment—he most completely *is* in the act of giving his life away" [I, 166].

As an example, he points to the French soldiers in the early days of World War I I who answered a call they felt deep within themselves to defend their country, knowing full well that they faced almost certain death [I, 167]. Yet they "died at peace with themselves," he declares, for they felt that answering that call was the most meaningful and fulfilling thing they could do in their terrible situation. Although they can not know what effect, if any, their sacrifices might have, those who are willing to give themselves to some cause do not judge their acts to be meaningless or to result in a total loss but to be "the summit, the culminating peak, of what we call their lives" [I, 167]. Needless to say, from a physical perspective it is nonsense to say that anyone achieves fulfillment by becoming a corpse. Their self-fulfillment, then, Marcel reasons, must occur at an "invisible," that is, spiritual level which "completely transcends the categories of biology." Whether such people explicitly believe in their survival after death or not, they lived and acted as though "death might be really, and in a supreme sense, life" *[I, 167]*. "Whether or not he actually believes in eternal life, the person who sacrifices himself acts as if he believed," Marcel writes in *Creative Fidelity*,[10] for, to repeat, such persons experience their acceptance of the call to give their lives, not as ending in total failure or annihilation, but as the most meaningful and fulfilling thing they can do.

Of course, those who offer their lives for a cause may be unable to articulate, even to themselves, exactly what they live for and they may never even ask about the nature or origin of the call they respond to. "The truth is," Marcel says, "that in the last analysis I do not know [clearly and distinctly] what I live by nor why I live" *[I, 167]*. Elsewhere, he admits that from a religious point of view, the person of faith may claim it is God who is calling for self-sacrifice[11] but, on a purely philosophical level, the call's origin and nature are not at all clear. What must a cause, such as peace or justice or freedom, be that one could feel called to give his or her life to defend and promote it? Surely it could not be just an abstract value or formula; would anyone be willing to die for an abstraction? (We might recall that in Chapter 4 Marcel asked, what is truth that someone would be willing to die for it? No one ever died for an abstract definition, he replied, and he wondered if truth might be a person.[12]) But he does not pursue these issues at this time; he will return to them in Volume II.

Not only do I not know clearly or in detail the nature of the goal I strive for, I also do not fully know my own life. "My life infinitely transcends my possible conscious grasp of my life at any moment" *[I, 167]*, Marcel states, and as a result our lives may be "strangers to their own underlying depths" *[I, 169]*. I believe he is pointing to the fact that I am not clearly aware of many features of my life, such as my deepest fears, loves, desires, memories (especially painful ones)—all that some psychologists place in my subconscious. Likewise, I do not have clear

---

10   CF, 77.

11   TW, 67-69.

12   *I*, 58, 72.

and precise knowledge of the deepest call within me, the call of my vocation or my ideal self. Therefore, although practical situations may force me to undertake a moral evaluation of my life, any such evaluation may be erroneous *[I, 168]*. Elsewhere he suggests that our situation in relation to our ideal self or being is analogous to the artist's relation to the creative idea which guides him or her.[13] Artists cannot explicitly define or describe the idea that they attempt to embody in a work of art even though they continually use it as a model to evaluate and adjust their creations. Similarly, we cannot define or describe exactly our vocation or ideal self which guides us, although we constantly use its light to evaluate and modify our lives.[14] And, the task of philosophy, Marcel suggests, may be to discover the conditions under which my true vocation and my real moral status may emerge at least in a partial and temporary way. (From what he said at the beginning of this chapter, such conditions would ultimately have to involve an absolute Thou.) As an illustration, he cites a character in his play *The Broken World* who through "the light of secondary reflection" finally comes to glimpse "the truth within her deepest nature" *[I, 169]* and to recognize that a false self ("soul") has been animating her life. All of us, he concludes, need the recuperative power of secondary reflection[15] to plumb the true depths of ourselves, but that reflection can be undertaken only with the mediation of others. That serves as his transition to the next lecture where he will discuss, among other things, interpersonal, or in his term, intersubjective, relations.

Pages in other works which treat material of this chapter:
CF, 47-54, 66-67, 77-78, 144-46, 167-69.
HV, 20-25.   CA, 191-94.   BH, 124-25.

---

13   *MB, II, 117;* HV, 25.

14   EBHD, 86-88, 95, where he says that the light which guides us cannot be conceptualized or made into an idea.

15   Since Marcel calls reflection on my self secondary reflection here, and it seems clearly to be what he called recollection in Chapter 7, he must believe that recollection is or involves some form of secondary reflection.

9

TOGETHERNESS: IDENTITY AND DEPTH

In this chapter, Marcel discusses two topics: intersubjective relations (the "togetherness" of the title) and the nature of one's personal identity though time. Let me say right in the beginning of my commentary, that I find some of his treatment of the second topic rather obscure, particularly insofar as it involves the notion of "depth."

He begins by returning to the question "Who am I?" and reviewing many points from previous chapters [I, 171]. It is impossible, he repeats, for me to give an "objective" answer to that question for I cannot be a detached observer and view my self as an object external to me. Nor can anyone else give a valid answer since I myself would have to confer on them their right to do so. Besides, he repeats from the end of the last chapter, my life is "essentially ungraspable," for it "infinitely transcends my possible conscious grasp" of it "at any given moment" [I, 167]. Nevertheless, as he said earlier, I can be called upon to sacrifice or consecrate it to some cause and doing so may be the natural culmination of a life which has been dedicated to that cause. Now that act of self-dedication, he continues, is not something that comes to my life from *outside*, rather it is "from the very depths of my own life" that an inner demand or exigency drives me to dedicate my self. (Recall in earlier chapters, he said that it is within the *deep* regions of myself that I find my being, my ideal self, and experience the call or vocation, even the obligation, to consecrate my life to a cause.) Furthermore, as we saw in the last chapter, even though human life is driven from within to dedicate itself to something, that "something" must be "something other than itself" [I, 176]. Therefore, since we are investigating life from a phenomenological point of view, that is, as I myself consciously live and experience it and not as something to be studied objectively (as in biology), it is reasonable for me to ask myself what sense (*sens*), if any, it has. (Marcel points out that the French word *sens*, translated as sense, contains the notions of both meaning and direction [I, 172].)[1] Even if I deny my life has any sense, the fact I raise the question implies that it could have some, at least in some cases.

---

1   The translator often renders *sens* as "point." I prefer to stick with the English cognate sense.

When I wonder about its sense, Marcel goes on, I might be presuming my life has direction and meaning in itself, whether I want it to or not. It would be as if I had a part assigned to me in a play and, if the play as a whole has a plot or theme, so will my life. The problem is that no producer has told me my part nor even what the rough outline of the overall plot of the play is. Naturally, then, "at first glance" I might suspect that there is no producer nor a play with a plot and thus that my life has no point and is meaningless *[I, 173]*.

To counter its apparent meaninglessness, I might wonder whether I myself could give my life some meaning and direction.[2] However, this would mean, he states, that the act which gives my life sense would be external to it, since in itself or intrinsically my life would have no meaning. Marcel rejects that by repeating that the act by which I consecrate my life to some cause springs from within my self, from my inner need for self-dedication mentioned earlier and that act "resembles the bursting of my life into flower" *[I, 174]*. Although his words are unexplained, I believe he is referring here to his previous chapter where he argued that a life dedicated to a cause is perceived by the dedicated person as a response to a call from deep within and also that he or she believes, at least implicitly, that that response is meaningful since through it he or she attains fulfillment ("the bursting of my life into flower").

Another reason Marcel gives for rejecting the view that we ourselves can create sense for our lives is that our existence precedes our awareness of ourselves and, just as our lives are given to us, so too we have "inherited" all kinds of meaning and direction "conferred upon us" by the world "in which we participate" *[I, 175]*. To understand what he means we must draw out the implications of his earlier notions of situation and participation, he says. Recall that in Chapter 7, he insisted that I am immersed in (participate in) my particular situation in the world like in a womb which means my surroundings significantly affect me, both physically and mentally. In this present chapter he decides to focus on the participation involved in "the relationships between myself and others" and how they affect me *[I, 175]*.

To do so, he begins by presenting a condensed version of his analysis in Chapter I of *Homo Viator*. In that chapter, entitled "The Ego and its Relations to Others," Marcel explains that by the term ego he does not mean an isolated entity with precise boundaries but a part of myself

---

2   As Marcel notes, that is the position of atheistic existentialists like Jean-Paul Sartre, *I, 174-75.*

which I focus on and present to others for their recognition and approval.[3] Because it is exposed and vulnerable, I want to safeguard my ego from all external threats, especially from being ignored or slighted by others [I, 176]. However, for me to concentrate on my ego is idolatry of myself, he claims, for I consider myself to be the privileged "center of my universe and see others either as obstacles to be overcome or as mirrors to reflect back to me a favorable image of my self."[4] Here, in *The Mystery of Being* [I, 177] he offers the example of a shy young man at a party who is extremely self-conscious because he knows no one and feels himself at the mercy of the gazes of others. Such self-centeredness, which views others as objects which threaten one's ego, is the opposite of an intersubjective (subject to subject, not subject to object) relation with others.

It might be appropriate here to say a brief word about the meaning of the term subject for Marcel. A subject is always contrasted to an object or thing and often the word is used interchangeably with self or I or person. A more specific meaning was given in Chapter 5 where "myself as subject" meant the permanent, noncontingent dimension of my self, the unique self I always am no matter how much I change [I, 86-87]. In Volume II[5] Marcel indicates that by a subject he means a self insofar as it has an inner life of its own, that is, insofar as it is aware of itself as a source of conscious acts (knowing, willing, desiring, wondering, and so forth) that asks itself what am I and what should I be, and a self that is aware that by its free choices and actions it lives its own life. Perhaps most important, a subject for Marcel is a being which possesses intrinsic value and so, as he said above, has traditionally been considered sacred [I, 87].

An intersubjective relation, then, is a relation of subjects or selves who to some degree recognize each other as unique, free, self-conscious beings who possess intrinsic value and who are, or should be, in charge of the sense and direction of their lives. Even more, intersubjectivity is a relation where the subject I am is truly *with* other subjects, Marcel says. Objects such as a chair and a table can be beside but never really *with* each other, since that preposition signifies a "bond" between subjects [I, 177]. Intersubjectivity is a relation between subjects that "really does

3   HV, 14-20.

4   HV, 19-20.

5   II, 25, 55-57.

bind" [*I, 181*] and unite subjects together "at the ontological level, that is *qua* beings" [*I, 178*] so that they "negate themselves as simple, detached items" [*I, 181*], that is, as isolated individuals. One way he characterizes this union is to call it an "internal" one, meaning that it "makes a difference to both of us." Of course, things can act on each other and thereby make a difference to each other, but only externally. Subjects in an intersubjective union also affect each other internally, in each other's thoughts and feelings, their self-understanding and self-evaluation, as well as their choices about the direction and sense of their lives. Since, as we shall see shortly, there is a range of intersubjective relations from the practical to profound love, the influence of subjects on each other also varies. To state the obvious, persons with whom I am most intimately bound, such as my spouse, children, and close friends, have a tremendous effect on all that I am internally and externally.

One of Marcel's preferred ways of referring to an intersubjective relation is to call it an I-thou, rather than an I-him or her or it relation [*I, 179*]. As we noted above when speaking of an absolute Thou, the English word "thou" is used to translate the familiar and intimate form of the pronoun you in French, *tu* not *vous*,[6] thereby indicating again that intersubjectivity is an intimate union of two subjects, not a subject object relation. Yet even to speak of the intersubjective bond as an I-thou relation is, at least verbally, to separate the I from the thou, he remarks, and so in *Creative Fidelity* in order to emphasize their union he affirms "the indistinctness of the I and the thou"[7] and states that an intersubjective relation transcends the "categories of the same and the other."[8] That is, subjects joined together in intersubjective relations do not fuse into one and the *same* being, nor on the other hand do they remain totally separate to each other as "two nuclei quite distinct from each other." They are truly united in a "suprapersonal unity" [*I, 182*], yet the integrity of each person is not obliterated in their unity but enhanced, for their relationship is "fructifying" and a "vital milieu" from which each subject "draws its strength," Marcel states.[9] Experience

---

6   The English translation occasionally misses that important difference. For example, on *I, 182 Toi-meme* (ME, I, 197) is translated as You when it should be Thou.

7   CF, 35.

8   CF, 34.

9   CF, 35.

confirms what he says for I do feel strengthened and enhanced by my intersubjective union with others whether it be simply working together in a common project or the most intimate form of love.[10] Most clearly in love, our beings are expanded by sharing or participating in each other's lives and experiences; if a person with whom I am lovingly united is sad or discouraged, I share those feelings; if that person is joyful and hopeful, so am I. In fact, to some degree, depending on the strength of their bond, selves in *every* intersubjective relation, even those that are purely practical in nature, share their pains and pleasures, their hopes and fears, their successes and disappointments, just as they join together their mutual quests for certain goals.

In addition, since in an intersubjective relationship the other person is not a threat or obstacle but supportive of me, I am able to relax my egocentric concentration on myself [I, 178] and become open and available to the calls, explicit or implicit, of many others [I, 179]. That openness, Marcel says, may result in genuine intimate communication between us, where we reveal our true selves to each other, which, I think, is what he is referring to when he states that "all human intercourse worthy of the name takes place in an atmosphere of real intimacy" [I, 182].

In ordinary experience, Marcel observes, there is a whole range of intersubjective relations, from, at the lowest level, people joining together for some "strictly practical" goal to, at the highest level, "the mystical communion of souls in worship" [I, 178]. Yet even in the first case, workers at a common task may have a real feeling of companionship and community if they are aware of each other as subjects sharing a common situation and of the unique contribution each makes to their common goal [I, 180]. Indeed, the briefest encounter, such as asking someone for directions, may have, he says, a "touch of genuine intersubjectivity" if the person I ask identifies with me to some degree, "by putting himself ... in my shoes" [I, 179] and showing genuine concern for me.

Not only do intersubjective relations take place between different subjects, they also exist "within the life of the one subject" he claims. "In its own intrinsic structure," Marcel states, "subjectivity is already, and in the most profound sense, genuinely intersubjective" [I, 182].

10   On *I, 188* Marcel says that love is the most intimate form of intersubjectivity. Also in the second volume, he states that "intersubjectivity is nothing but charity itself" indicating that all such relations contain love to some degree [II, 170].

Again, this is not to say that I am a plurality of subjects for "unity and plurality are yoked together within the borders of the unique being that I am" [I, 183]. He refers, for example, to the relation between my past self and my present self within the one being that I am when he asks to what extent "can my relationship with my own past" be represented objectively? That provokes a further question, in what sense do we still bear our past? Of course, by using our memory we are able to fill out a dossier or questionnaire about our past life taken as a whole but that inevitably distorts it, he says, since it treats our past like an object detached from, and external to, us. The more we still live our past experience, that is, the more it remains part of us, the less we can detach ourselves from it [I, 183-84]. Those different ways of viewing our past, as separate from or as a part of ourselves,[11] force us to recognize that we *are* our past "in a very uneven way," Marcel says, just as we are our present unevenly. Since our present moods and attitudes change, that means that the way we understand and evaluate our past changes. (He made the same point in the previous chapter when talking about our lives.) Therefore, we cannot consider our past as if it is preserved or fixed once and for all. Furthermore, there are moments in the present when I actually relive my past experiences, such as the fears I felt as an eight year old boy when my parents were late and the pain I felt in high school upon the death of a close friend. Does that mean, he asks, that I still am in some sense that boy and that high school student? The answer, he replies, is both yes and no [I, 184].

On the one hand, I am not still the boy or teenager in the sense that my eight year old self or my teenage self are like physical objects which continue to be the same over many years, as do the photographs taken of me as a child. Yet in another sense, Marcel stresses, I must still be that boy and that teenager, since their "modes of existence ... are not objectifiable" [I, 185], that is, they cannot be treated as objects separate from me because they can be resurrected and relived by my present self. If I am able to relive experiences of my past self, they and it must still be part of me in some way. In fact, Marcel goes on, there is "an innumerable multiplicity of presences"[12] [I, 185], that is, forms of my self, that

---

11 Note that the difference indicates the workings of primary and secondary reflection respectively.

12 My translation from ME, I, 200. Marcel will discuss his notion of presence in the next chapter.

enter into all kinds of relations with my present self. In addition to my present self, I am also the self I was yesterday (or years ago) as well as the self I desire to be and those selves can really struggle with each other as, for instance, when I strive in the present to overcome bad habits I built up in my past self in order to become the better self I should be in the future. Does the multiplicity of forms of my self mean that I must deny that I possess a "continuing personal identity" [I, 185], he asks? Must I say that, because I am multiple selves which continually change, I am *not* now the same individual person who was once an eight year old boy and then a teenage adolescent and, furthermore, that the self which comes to be ten years, or ten months, from now will not be the same person that I am now? To answer this, he says, we must investigate the "notion of personal identity and ... how we are to understand it" [I, 185].

Judgments of identity, Marcel contends, strictly apply to the world of tangible things; for example, the watch I find this afternoon has the identical description of the one I lost this morning [I, 185-86]. Yet even in the case of physical objects, there can be complications. When, over time, I have replaced every single part of my watch, can I still say it is the same watch I purchased two years ago? In fact, why would I consider it to be the same, except that there is what Marcel calls a *"felt quality of identity"* which, he states, is "in its very nature not objectifiable" [I, 187] which means, of course, that it must be part of me in some way. His next example provides a good illustration. A child might consider her favorite doll to be the same even though every one of its parts had been replaced over time. The doll remains the same to the child, he explains, because its new parts have been taken up into the unity of the child's "sense of possession and almost of adoration ... for this especially beloved object" [I, 187]. In other words, even though all of the doll's parts have in fact changed, the child has the same strong feelings of possession and affection for that "new" doll that she did for the original one. Of course, along with the permanence of such feelings, or "felt quality of identity," in the child, there is also an actual historical continuity between the original doll and the present one. What complicates things, he points out, is that historical continuity between objects may be present even when the felt quality of permanence is lacking in the subject.[13] To illustrate he uses the example of meeting someone whom he is certain is

---

13   The English translation says "permanence of a felt quality in the object" (I, 187). However, the words "in the object" are not in the French (ME, I, 202),

a person who was a classmate of his years ago, yet who now does not provoke in him any feelings of identity that would confirm that he is the same person.[14] That difference, he argues, highlights the contrast made earlier between viewing someone as a he, she, or it (an object) and as a thou, a subject with whom I have an intimate intersubjective bond.[15] In the second case, especially when I encounter those I have really loved, I can have the feeling that they are the same thous even when I reencounter them after a long period of time, even if I were to meet them after death [I, 187-88]! The reason I feel that an individual I reencounter is the same thou is, of course, that we have continued to be bound together intimately.

The gap between the objective identity we can affirm in the world of things and the felt quality of identity forces us, Marcel says, to acknowledge again "a kind of manifoldness within the self" [I, 188] and that prompts him to return to the issue of personal identity. "At the level of feeling, quality ... encroaches upon the subject itself,"[16] he states, and he tries to explain what he means by distinguishing between seeing a color and feeling a pain. "One can make a distinction," he says, "between seeing a color and the color one sees, but not between feeling a pain and the pain one feels. The felt pain is an indissoluble unity" [I, 188]. To understand what he means, we need to remind ourselves once again that Marcel proceeds as a phenomenologist and so by pain he means the *experience* or *feeling* of pain, not some biological description of it. Thus, for him to state that the feeling of pain and the pain itself are "an

---

nor should they be, since Marcel says the "felt quality of identity" is "in its very nature not objectifiable" (I, 189).

14 The English translation (I, 187) is misleading because it adds words not in the French edition and omits some that are (ME, I, 202-03). The English has "There was nothing [in the quality of these two appearances nor in my feelings about them] that could confirm that [they were two appearances of] the same person." I have bracketed the words not in the French text. A strict translation of the French would be, "There was nothing *in me* that could confirm that *it was* the same person." I have italicized words omitted from the English translation.

15 Once again the English translation fails to capture the intimacy present in Marcel's French text (ME, I, 263) by translating *toi* as the impersonal you rather than as thou in the following sentence: "So it is you [*toi*], so it is really you [*toi*]" (MB, I, 187).

16 My translation from ME, I, 204.

indissoluble unity" makes perfect sense for what is pain experientially if not the feeling of pain?

However, other than repeating we must not interpret feelings or sensations as a transmission of signals, Marcel does not clearly explain how the above remarks apply to the issue of personal identity, although he claims they do. Let me propose that he is suggesting that, just as pain and the feeling of pain cannot be distinguished, so too I cannot distinguish or make a distinction between my feeling of my personal identity through time from the personal identity I feel across time [I, 188]. Just as my felt pain is an indissoluble unity, so my felt personal identity is an indissoluble unity. It is true that I can distinguish my feeling that the Paul I meet today is the same Paul I knew forty years ago, from Paul himself; in fact, I could be wrong, he may not be the same Paul. Error is possible because of the aforementioned gap between objective identity (Paul himself) and the "felt quality of identity" I experience (that is, my feeling that the person before me is the Paul I knew forty years ago). However, when it comes to my self, Marcel seems to be stating that no distinction can be made between my feeling my own personal identity and the personal identity of myself that I feel; there is no gap between them. That is, since as phenomenologists we are investigating experience (in this case my experience that I am still in some sense the young boy and the teenager I was in the past, even though over the years I have changed significantly), my feeling that I am still the same person that I was in the past *is* my personal identity felt by me across time.

Next he proceeds to work out the implications of these remarks for our understanding of our personal identity. For one thing, I cannot represent my life as a sequence of images which succeed each other on a film or video tape. That is because, "our inner experience, as we live that experience," in other words, our felt experience of being fundamentally the same unique person throughout our lives, "would be an impossibility for a being who was merely a succession of images" [I, 189]. If one image merely replaced another, nothing permanent would endure. Besides, Marcel notes, even a succession of images, one replacing another, is known to be a succession only by a consciousness that is aware that it itself endures through time and so is aware of one image passing out of view and being succeeded by the next, which passes out of view and is succeeded by the next, and so on. He repeats, neither the "feeling" of our personal identity, nor our life "as it is experienced from the inside" can "be translated into terms of film" [I, 190]. Does this mean we must represent "the inner reality of my life as something static and invariable?" No, he responds, for everything in the world, including my inner reality, changes. We are forced, then, "to envisage the necessity of transcending the opposition," Marcel states, "between the endless changing flow and the static" if "we want to remain loyal to the data of experience" [I, 191]. That data is that I am not static but continually change, and yet I never change so much that I cease being the particular individual I am (Gabriel Marcel) and turn into someone else (Jean-Paul Sartre). As he puts it more abstractly, "human life ... will not really let itself be represented as a purely successive phenomena, there being something in its structure [namely one's personal identity] that is not properly compared to a succession of images." In order to go beyond the opposition between endless flux and static immutability, we need a new "spiritual" category, he states.

That will involve, he adds rather abruptly, perceiving how life can be linked with truth; in fact, he claims, we have been trying to discover that link since we first discussed truth in Chapter 4 [I, 191]. However, he goes on, that linkage cannot really be shown to us now for it lies in a dimension of reality beyond life, "that of depth itself" [I, 192]. Depth, he says, can be discovered at many levels, but especially at the level of one's own life when life is not looked upon as a mere succession of images or a story. That seems to indicate that depth is the new spiritual category he introduces in order to explain our personal identity, a category which transcends the opposition between pure succession and static immutability.

Marcel uses a portion of his 1938 journal (now published as *Presence and Immortality*) to clarify his notion of depth. Our experience of depth, he explains, "seems to be linked ... to the feeling that a promise is being made," although at present we can only catch a "glimpse" of "the fulfillment of the promise" [I, 192]. We are striving for that fulfillment, he declares, as for a homeland we are tied to, but in exile from, and homesick for. Although he doesn't say so, I suspect that the fulfillment he refers to here is the fulfillment of our urgent inner demand for an experience both pure and full of intelligibility and truth that he described in Chapter 3 and which he claimed was the impetus behind the philosophical search. If I am correct, then Marcel is claiming here that in my experience of the depth of my life I experience or feel a promise being made that my demand for fulfillment will be met—because I somehow, even now, catch a glimpse of that fulfillment. To put it another way, I experience in my depths, albeit obscurely, the link between life (and its demand for fulfillment) and truth (which is that fulfillment) that he referred to above.

Our experience of depth, Marcel goes on, is also an experience that the future is in harmony with the past; indeed, that "in the dimension of depth the past and the future firmly embrace" in a region which he calls "the present,"[17] which is an "absolute Here-and Now" beyond time and which "could be nothing other than eternity" [*I, 194*].

If we combine his remarks about depth, we find Marcel claiming that the experience of depth is an experience of a promise that our demand for fulfillment will be met in a realm beyond time, a realm of an eternal present. And I experience that promise because, even now, I somehow catch a glimpse of that realm and that fulfillment. Needless to say, that is quite a claim, and I will attempt to make some sense of it after we see how he uses the notion of depth to explain our personal identity throughout our lives.

Marcel originally introduced the notion of depth in his discussion of personal identity when he was looking for a new spiritual category which transcended the opposition between an endless flow of successive states and the static or immutable. The concept of depth, he now says, allows us to glimpse how "the opposition of the successive, as such, and the abstract, as such [viz. the unchanging], can be transcended at a supratemporal level which is," he states, "the very depth of time" [*I, 194*]. I believe that "supratemporal level" is in the realm of the eternal he mentioned above and that it is, in fact, my personal identity. I say this because in an earlier work, *Being and Having*, he had written that "on a certain level I cannot fail to appear to myself ... as eternal."[18] Referring again to that level, he also wrote that I can distinguish within myself "a ruling principle which asserts its *identity across time* ... [and] *with which I identify myself*" from my continually changing states or "life-process" which the ruling principle transcends and tries to control.[19] In other words, for Marcel my depth is a supratemporal part (level) of my self

---

17 Unfortunately, this word in the French edition, ME, I, 209, is omitted in the English translation (I, 194). I have also slightly modified other parts of the English translation.

18 BH, 20.

19 BH, 42. I have added the emphasis and slightly modified the English translation from the French edition, *Être et avoir* (Paris: Aubier, 1935), 57.

which transcends the continual temporal flow or succession of my states and because of that can be designated the eternal part of my self. It is the part of me "with which I identify myself" since it is my "identity across time" which I experience no matter how many changes I undergo, for I never change so radically that I cease to experience my self to be the same unique individual self I was in the past.

He also briefly suggests that my depth can be understood as my "essence or essential nature" as contrasted with my temporal changing "existence." My essence, he explains, is "that aspect [of my self] which we cannot disregard" [I, 195], which means, I presume, that my essence is that part of me which is most fundamentally me, for it is what I always am no matter how much I change. If that is correct, then for Marcel my essence is the eternal, supratemporal, depth dimension of my self, the permanent self I am throughout my life history.[20]

Marcel concludes this chapter by remarking that as people get older, they nearly always have a feeling they are growing nearer to their childhood, that is, to a state of "being still the object of protective care and tender guidance" [I, 195], a state they feel in exile from and homesick for. His repetition of the terms exile and homesick suggests he has in mind what he referred to earlier as a state of fulfillment where our exigency for transcendence would be satisfied and that brings us back to his assertion that in our experience of depth we experience a promise that our inner demand for fulfillment will be satisfied in an eternal realm, a promise that arises from the fact that we can even now catch a glimpse of that realm.

Let me finish my commentary on Chapter 9 by offering some suggestions as to how we might understand Marcel's rather astonishing claim that we are able this side of death to glimpse the eternal realm of our fulfillment. In Chapter 8 he argued that those who respond to a call from their *depths* to sacrifice their lives for a cause feel, at least implicitly, that in doing so they are being true to their ideal self and that in giving their lives they are not being annihilated but actually attaining fulfillment [I, 166-67]. Of course, as he said there, such fulfillment could only take place in a spiritual realm beyond time and death. Therefore, insofar as such individuals have some experience or feeling that their fulfillment will occur in a realm beyond this temporal world and death, I believe

---

20   In support of my interpretation, I would point out that in *MB, II* Marcel states that life "when looked at ... in its essence" has a certain "perennialness" (*II, 164*).

they can be said in Marcel's language to catch a glimpse of that eternal realm and a promise of fulfillment there. Of course, it would be only the deep supratemporal eternal part of themselves, their permanent essential selves, that could continue after death and achieve that fulfilment.

Finally, if we consider all of the foregoing within the context of his notion of participation, we can see another reason why Marcel claims we may glimpse in this life the eternal realm of our fulfillment. Because he believes we are in our depths supratemporal or eternal, I think that in his eyes we *already* partially transcend time and participate to some degree in an eternal realm that we are barely aware of this side of death. Since we already, albeit only partially and very imperfectly, participate in that realm where our demand for transcendence will be fulfilled, it is not unreasonable to suggest that we occasionally experience or glimpse that "homeland" which we are in exile from and homesick for. In *Homo Viator* in a Chapter entitled "Values and Immortality," he suggests that when we experience values which are essentially eternal (justice and love, for example, are always values), we catch a glimpse of our immortality in another world: "value is the mirror wherein it is given us to discern, always imperfectly and always through a distorting mist, the real face of our destiny...in another world."[21]

Pages in other works that treat material of this chapter:
HV, Chapter 1.   EBHD, 35-42, 83-90, 101-03.
PI, first entry.   CF, 32-36, 97-99.

---

21   HV, 153.

PRESENCE AS MYSTERY

M uch of the material in this last chapter of Volume I is not new. Although some terms, such as presence and mystery, are explained for the first time, we shall see that what they refer to has been discussed by Marcel in earlier chapters. Chapter 10 begins by briefly returning to the notion of depth, the supratemporal or eternal dimension of the self, the category proposed as an alternative to the opposition between total flux and total immutability. Since in this supratemporal dimension I transcend time, I must think of myself, he says, as more than "somebody thrust in the world at a [particular] moment of time." I must also think of myself as "bound to those who have gone before me" [I, 197], bound in an "obscure and intimate relationship"[1] that is more than just a causal one, that is, more than one where my ancestors simply form a long causal chain of which I am the most recent effect. Clearly for Marcel my intimate bonds with my ancestors are bonds of participation; in a later work he even states that my ancestors "are consubstantial with me and I with them."[2] It is from this perspective, he believes, that we should consider "the mystery of the family bond" which, he adds enigmatically, is "a particular expression of the general mystery of being," to which he will devote his second volume. Although we are talking about the family, we are not doing sociology, he maintains, because his philosophical investigation into the family still focuses on the central questions of this volume, "what am I?" and "how am I able to ask myself this question?". He, therefore, labels his approach "metasociological" [I, 197] and says it asks the same basic questions about our selves but now from a new perspective, from the perspective of our relationship to our family, present and past. In other words, we are asking, who or what am I as a self bound to (participating in) an extended family?

Marcel begins his discussion of the family bond by expressing his view that in today's world sonship and fatherhood lack the richness of

---

1   EBHD, 85.

2   Ibid.

meaning they had in other societies.[3] One reason for this, he suggests, is that the fact of being alive is not seen as "a value that allows us to think of life as a gift" *[I, 198]* and one reason for that is the tragic times in which we live.[4] Another reason for the decrease in meaning of the father/child relation is that in too many cases today fatherhood is the unintended result of reckless behavior by a man who refuses to accept responsibility for his offspring. A third reason is that the bond between parent and child is often viewed objectively as purely biological and so tends to "lose every spiritual quality" *[I, 197]*.

The only basis on which we can reject a nihilistic view of life and recognize it as a gift is, Marcel proposes, "in the name of a sort of 'depth' of reality which the nihilism refuses to recognize" *[I, 199-200]* and it is that depth that he was trying to set forth in his work *Homo Viator*. There he wrote that the "procreative instinct" can be experienced as a vocation, that is, as a call through which "an individual is in some way commanded to immolate his immediate personal aims"[5] and "place himself at life's disposal."[6] Yet that call can be recognized only if one welcomes life with gratitude and confidence because he or she views it as "a gift we have received."[7] One who experiences life as a gift will respond to its call, embodied in the procreative instinct, by accepting his responsibility for his offspring and committing himself to remain faithful to them. Such a commitment or vow, he states, is a spiritual act which is most essential to real fatherhood *[I, 201-02]* and it is that vow which a purely objective biological or scientific account of procreation ignores or eliminates *[I, 202-03]*. Needless to say, the family is normally

---

3   Much of what he says would, of course, apply also to mothers and daughters. One reason he gives for concentrating on fatherhood is that men do not have the close physical bonds with their children that women do and that allows him to focus more on the *spiritual* relationship involved in parenthood, HV, 102-04.

4   Remember that these lectures are given during the Cold War and in the early years of the nuclear arms race between the United States and the Soviet Union, just before the outbreak of the Korean War.

5   HV, 106. The chapter in HV which he has in mind is Chapter 4, "The Creative Vow as Essence of Fatherhood."

6   HV, 114.

7   HV, 115.

the concrete "incarnation" of a person's commitment to life.[8] To claim that commitment is the essence of fatherhood does not mean that we should "make a radical distinction between spiritual and biological fatherhood" Marcel says; for a "fullness of life" *[I, 202]* they should be together; after all we are embodied subjects, even embodied spirits, at the "juncture ... of the vital and spiritual" *[I, 203]*. Accordingly, even though adoption contains the spiritual commitment to a child, it too must be embodied in material acts of care and service.[9]

May I suggest that the major question about Marcel's analysis so far is whether he is justified in claiming that at a certain depth of reality, life is a value and a gift. He himself raises similar questions at the end of this chapter *[I, 218-19]* but does not suggest any answers; however, the question will be posed again in Volume II and there he will defend his view. For now, he returns to his reflections on the family bond and its mysterious character. He has chosen to emphasize that bond, he explains, in order to distinguish his conception of the human subject from those of other philosophers who view it as by nature independent of, or even isolated from, other subjects *[I, 204]*. From its beginning, every human subject is intersubjective, he insists, for we all come into existence within the most basic intersubjective relationship which consists of some kind of a family.

Because he has referred to the family bond as a mystery, Marcel next turns his attention to "this new and difficult notion" *[I, 204]*. (As we shall see, while the terminology is new, what it refers to is not.) One of the key characteristics of a mystery, he states, is that I am *within* it, or, to use earlier language, it is something in which I participate. Any attempt, then, to grasp it simply from the outside is bound to fail for a mystery is "*our* situation, the situation we cannot get outside of." For example, the family can be studied by sociology or history as an object, such as a social institution separate from me, and some truths about it can be discovered. However, since from birth I have been immersed in some kind of family, I can gain greater insight into its inner reality as a lived and experienced intersubjective relationship, by describing it "from inside," that is, by describing my lived experience of it, as a novelist would do.

---

8   HV, 85.

9   Marcel and his wife had no biological children but did adopt a young boy.

Perhaps, Marcel continues, we can most quickly arrive at the definition of a mystery by working out the distinction between an object and
a presence. As we have noted many times, he uses the term object to
refer to something that is separate and distinct from the subject. An
object is also something on which I can perform "a whole set of practical
operations" that are generally communicable [I, 205]. A presence is quite
different and to illustrate that difference he points out that someone
who is physically near us may be much less present to us than a loved
one thousands of miles away who is continually in our thoughts and
affections. No doubt we can more easily physically communicate with
the former individual but he is "not really present to us" because we are
not in "communion" with him [I, 205]. The word communion is crucial
and should remind us of his earlier treatment of participation and intersubjectivity where he stressed the intimate bond or union involved in
an I-thou, as distinct from an I-him or I-her, relation. Because presence
involves a union of subjects we can say of it what Marcel said about
intersubjectivity in Chapter 9, those in such a union are affected and
affect each other *internally* in their thoughts, feelings, self-understanding, goals, and so forth.[10] He refers to that internal effect here when he
remarks that someone's presence, when it makes itself felt, "can refresh
my inner being ... [and] it makes me more fully myself than I would be
if I were not exposed to its impact" [I, 205]. We all know from experience how we gain renewed self-esteem and energy when others join
with us and share our efforts. Their presence to us, their participation
in our lives, may strengthen us so much that we can achieve goals that
we would not even attempt on our own—including the goal of living
up to our ideal self or vocation.

Since a presence is not an object, the attitude by which we approach
it must be essentially different, Marcel indicates, from the attitude by
which we approach an object. An object can literally be grasped, physically or mentally, and manipulated, but a presence can only be "welcomed
or rebuffed" [I, 208]. The term welcome was used earlier when he was
explaining his notion of active receptivity in Chapter 6.[11] Applying some
of that analysis here, we could say that we must approach a presence
with an active effort to be open and receptive to it, especially when the
presence in question is that of another person. It is interesting, however,

10   *I, 178-82.*

11   *I, 117-19.*

that Marcel also speaks here of nonhuman things as presences, under certain conditions. For example, a poem is able to magically evoke the presence of a rose to us *[I, 208]*. Recall that earlier he distinguished between an objective approach to a flower by a scientist and the creative participatory approach of an artist.[12] To experience a rose as a presence, he explains, is different from viewing it as an object separate from me that I can classify (as in botany) or manipulate for practical ends (such as the making of perfume). The poem, through its words, is somehow able to help me become open and receptive to the reality of the rose itself and appreciate and welcome it just as the beautiful flower that it is. In that case, the rose is not an object before me but part of my very being; in other words, the rose is a presence in which I participate and because we are united, the rose affects me *internally*, for example, it may refresh me by its beauty, it may help me realize that nonhuman things can be intrinsically valuable, it may prompt me to care more for the natural world.

One concrete example of presence that Marcel does discuss in some detail is illness. To treat illness from an objective point of view is to regard it from the outside as "the breakdown of an apparatus," the malfunctioning of an organism. To recognize illness as a presence is to see it from the inside as affecting "the being of the person who is ill" and who has to choose "his attitude towards it" *[I, 209]*. That is, a person with a serious illness must decide how to live with it. Will he give up, use his illness as a reason to rebel against God or fate, use it to gain pity from others, or see it as a battle to be fought or as an ordeal which provides him an opportunity to grow in patience, courage, and faith *[I, 211]*? Insofar as I (or others) recognize my illness as a presence, that is, as part of me, as something in which I participate, I thereby "recognize my illness as a mystery," Marcel asserts *[I, 210]*. Similarly, to perceive another's illness as a mystery is to see it as a presence and thus as part of his or her very being and that is to view the person not primarily as a malfunctioning organism but as an ill "neighbor" who calls me to be "compassionate and helpful" *[I, 210]*; in other words, who calls me to an intersubjective union of love with him. We can even interpret death as "a mystery and not a mere objective event" *[I, 211]*, he contends, meaning that it too is a presence which is part of me, affects me internally, and is something I must decide how to live with. (He promises more discussion of death in Volume II.)

12 *I, 120-21.*

After giving concrete illustrations of presences and mysteries, Marcel offers a general definition of the difference between a problem and a mystery, quoting from *Being and Having [I, 211]*. To view something as a problem is to perceive it as an object that is before me which I can in principle control and manipulate (at least mentally) by some technique and use to attain some end. (Of course, primary reflection is a tool of the problematic approach.) A mystery, however, is something in which I am involved and participate and so I should not attempt to treat it as if I were a detached spectator of it. Because a mystery is joined to my being, the relationship involved, he says, transcends the distinction between what is totally inside of me and what is altogether outside of me as an object. (May I point out, that is the same point he made earlier when discussing participation.) Yet a mystery can be degraded and turned into a problem; it can even be ignored or actively denied and he mentions the so-called problem of evil. To treat evil as a problem is to view it as an object outside of me, for example, as a defect in a living organism and thus to ignore or deny my involvement in it. To treat evil as a mystery is to see it as a presence, as part of my being, and so to see myself as participating in it and having to take up an attitude toward it.

Furthermore, the mysterious is not simply negative, that is, something which I cannot know and so might as well forget about. Rather, "the recognition of mystery," Marcel states, "is an essentially positive act of the mind" *[I, 212]* in which I become aware (and, so, know in some sense) that I am "the beneficiary of an intuition which I possess without immediately knowing myself to possess it" *[I, 212]*.[13] That intuition was mentioned earlier when, at the end of Chapter 2, he stated that all reflection bases itself on an "intuition of supra-reflective unity" *[I, 38]* which enables secondary reflection to critique the divisions that result from primary reflection.[14] I would suggest that the intuition he speaks of is my basic *immediate nonreflective awareness* or experience of my union with, or submerged participation in, all the many realities Marcel has discussed in this first volume—my body and the sensible world, my particular situation, my life, my vocation, other human subjects, especially

---

13   My translation from, ME, I, 228.

14   As I noted earlier, I believe that the intuition is also referred to when he speaks of my feeling of my own body as a "*nonmediatizable immediate*" (*I, 109*) and of sensation as immediate awareness of the world (MJ, 320, 329).

my family; in other words, everything that is a presence to me. Thus, "the recognition of mystery" that he refers to above is my conscious act of reflection by which I explicitly become aware that I participate in those realities. That awareness comes only through secondary reflection on my basic immediate nonreflective experience or intuition which, since it is nonreflective, is not self-conscious and, therefore, as he says, "can grasp itself only through the modes of experience in which it is reflected" *[I, 212]*.[15]

Marcel then goes on to apply the mystery/problem distinction to the difference between philosophy and science and in doing so repeats many points he made in his first chapter. It is theoretically possible, he states, that anyone can repeat mathematical proofs and the scientific experiments which establish the laws of nature. That is not the case with "existential [phenomenological] philosophy," however, for it is based on "various kinds of deep experiences" *[I, 213]*[16] which not everyone has or, at least, recognizes that they have. (The deep experiences he has in mind are, I imagine, experiences involving the ultimate questions about the self, life and death, meaning and meaninglessness, the presence or nonexistence of God, and so forth.) In addition, his philosophy is a response to a "kind of appeal" or a "kind of call" to the reader's "inner resources" *[I, 213]*, a call to each individual to reflect upon his or her most fundamental experiences and personally attempt to discover the truth about them. As he said in Chapter 1, each individual must personally live and be gripped by a philosophical question and seek his or her own response to it. Clearly, then, philosophy for Marcel deals with mysteries, that is, with aspects of reality in which I participate.

On the other hand, science, which deals with problems, attempts to discover solutions "that can become common property ... [and] at least in theory be rediscovered by anyone at all" *[I, 213]*, provided, of course, and this is a big proviso, they are able to understand and use the empirical methods of science.[17] As he asserted in Chapter 1, science is "lost in anonymity" *[I, 7]*, in the sense that the scientist acting as a scientist "is concerned with an order of truth [about the world] which he must

---

15 My translation from, ME, I, 228.

16 The word *inner* is not in the French, ME, I, 229.

17 Since in fact not everyone can understand or use the experimental methods of science, it is simply not the case that "anyone at all" can arrive at scientific conclusions.

consider as wholly outside of, and completely distinct from, his own self" *[I, 215]*. Thus, the individual features of the particular scientist must vanish as much as possible as he or she pursues "objective data" *[I, 216]*. However, now, in Chapter 10, Marcel acknowledges that he is talking only about the "elementary" level of science which can be taught to almost everyone. Science "at the very highest level" concerns itself with its own fundamental principles and thus enters the area of mystery, he admits *[I, 214]*. For example, many great scientists have sought to understand their discipline as a human endeavor of those who share certain basic presuppositions about the nature of reality and about the nature of the human mind that creates science.[18] Some scientists have wondered about the limitations of the scientific method and have asked if that method is in fact totally objective and value free. Some scientists explicitly raise questions about values, for example, about the morality of doing nuclear research or genetic engineering. Since scientists who raise such questions are asking about matters in which they themselves are personally involved, they are dealing with mysteries in Marcel's sense of the term and, at that level, he admits, "the line of demarcation between philosophy and the sciences tends to fade away" *[I, 214]*.

Because the philosopher deals with realities that are "present" to his or her self and "not really separable from it," it follows that there is "an organic connection between presence and mystery" *[I, 216]*. For Marcel every presence is mysterious for it is joined to the self in some way. He adds that it is doubtful that the term mystery can be properly used when a presence is not at least "making itself felt," for, again, a mystery is something in which the self is involved, something joined to its very being.

As a concrete illustration, Marcel points to the mysterious character of "the presence near one of a sleeping person, especially a sleeping child," and more generally of any vulnerable unprotected person *[I, 216]*. On the one hand, from the problematic point of view, such a person is simply an object completely in our power. However, if we approach the defenseless person as a mystery, that is, as a thou with whom we have an intimate union, we will see him or her as "sacred" *[I, 217]*, he says. Elsewhere, he explains that the sacred is "the mysterious principle at the

---

18   That is what Marcel is referring to as "determining the conditions" that make something like science possible (*I, 215*).

heart of human dignity"[19] and says it is based on belief in "the human soul created in the image of God" [II, 148]. Here, at the end of the first volume of *The Mystery of Being*, he links the sacred to "the essential" which he now defines as that which is absolutely at stake [I, 217]. To put this in terms of value, the essential is not valuable because it is a means to some end (Marcel calls that the important), but is absolutely valuable, as an end in itself. While the believer, on the basis of Divine Revelation, may name the essential "salvation," the philosopher, who has not "received the enlightenment of any special revelation" [I, 219], must ask whether on "a strictly philosophical level," one can affirm that there is something of absolute value or sacred at stake in human life [I, 218]. That question too, Marcel promises, will be addressed in his second volume.

In the final paragraphs of Chapter 10, Marcel vaguely hints that the essential, something of absolute value, may be found in the eternal, "transhistoric depth of history" [I, 218] and says we shall see later that there is a strict connection between the ideas of eternity and mystery. All that is left unexplained, but we might recall that in the previous chapter he discussed the supratemporal, eternal dimension of our selves, that deep part of us which is our personal identity throughout our personal history and in that sense is "transhistoric." Perhaps he is implying here that the eternal dimension of our selves is something of absolute value or sacred, for earlier he did suggest that the noncontingent self "with whom I am intimate" has traditionally been felt to possess a certain sacredness [I, 87]. He may also be suggesting that our eternal dimension participates in the eternal dimension of reality when he states that every mystery, which must mean every reality in which we participate, opens onto ("flows into") the eternal. That is true in some sense for each of us when it comes to our roots in our family, he says, for our historical "conditions under which we are inserted into the world" [I, 219][20] extend from our immediate family back into the mists of time to include innumerable unknown ancestors. (Some of these statements will become clearer in the second volume when Marcel focuses on the notion of being, for, as he said at the beginning of this chapter, "the mystery of the family bond" is "a particular expression of the general mystery of being" [I, 197].)

---

19 EBHD, 128; *Searchings*, 51.

20 My translation from ME, I, 235.

He concludes this series of lectures by asking again to what extent it is possible, without "the enlightenment of any special revelation," for us to raise ourselves above our condition as beings in the world and catch glimpses of a "higher sphere ... [of] fluctuating, glittering, unfixed lights that can to some degree throw light into the innermost depths of being?" [I, 219].[21] Since light is Marcel's metaphor for truth, he is apparently asking to what extent can we worldly beings glimpse truths about things beyond the physical world? I presume that in addition to truths about the innermost depth of being, those would also be truths that pertain to the sacredness of human beings, the essential, something of absolute value. These formidable issues,[22] he promises, will occupy him in Volume II and he prays that we who are seeking truth be granted help from "that Truth which is not a thing but a spirit" [I, 219].

May I point out, however, that in Chapter 9, Marcel has already claimed that in our experience of depth we experience a promise of fulfillment. We experience it, he stated, because we already catch "glimpses" beyond this temporal world of an eternal realm where our demand for fulfillment will be satisfied. In other words, to some extent he has already responded affirmatively to the question whether we are able to glimpse truths about a higher sphere beyond the physical world. He will say more about that higher sphere in Volume II.

Pages in other works that treat material of this chapter:
HV, Chapters 3 and 4.   EBHD, 81-90.
CF, 66-76.   CA, 178-81, 191-94.

---

21 My translation from ME, I, 235.

22 It must have been a slip of the pen for him to write "problem" on (*I*, 269) and ME, I, 235.

COMMENTATOR'S SUMMARY OF VOLUME I

Before moving on to Volume II, I want to offer a brief summary of what I believe are the major ideas Marcel has expounded in Volume I.

For one thing, he has stated that his philosophical approach is phenomenological, meaning that his procedure is to reflect upon and describe features of human life as we concretely live and experience them in order to grasp their essential characteristics. He calls the special instrument of philosophy secondary reflection. It seeks to go beneath and critique the divisions and separations introduced into experience by primary reflection and does so by returning to and entering deeply into our most basic prereflective experiences (also called intuitions) of our unity with, or participation in, all kinds of things, or, better, presences, such as my body, the world, my situation, my life, my vocation, all those with whom I am related intersubjectively. To say that philosophy deals with presences in which I participate is to say that it deals with mysteries.

We have also seen that Marcel considers the proper audience for philosophy to be those who experience a deep metaphysical uneasiness or anxiety about the fundamental conditions of their existence. That uneasiness prompts them to ask the ultimate questions, such as, is there a meaning to life?, what am I?, what am I truly worth?, is there a God?, is there life beyond death?, is there anything of absolute value? Philosophers are those who are driven by a deep inner demand for more open and receptive kinds of experience filled more and more with the light of truth and so containing some answer to those ultimate questions and, therefore, some satisfaction of their metaphysical uneasiness.

Finally, since the question who or what am I is so central to Volume I, I will attempt to weave together the various responses Marcel has offered to it. In the first place, although I am a single self I possess many different features, many of which I am not, or not fully, conscious of. Most fundamentally, I am in my depths a spiritual self that endures as the same unique self through time and is aware of doing so and, as such, I can be described as transhistorical, supratemporal and even eternal. Yet I am also a fundamentally incomplete and continually changing self with contingent and variable features. I am a self driven by a deep demand for ultimate truths about the fundamental nature of reality, including the nature of my self and my true moral worth. Yet I am also a self of desire and lust and fear who seeks to avoid truths that are challenging and painful. Although in my depths spiritual, I am also an embodied self in space and time whose felt existence is indubitable and is the central reference point for all sensed existents. As embodied I am naturally bound to the physical world which I experience (most basically by sensation) and to particular situations in that world and especially to other human subjects, first and foremost my extended family, and all of them form and mold me internally as well as externally. Thus, I am not an autonomous, self-sufficient, self-contained being, but one totally exposed and vulnerable to the physical and human worlds in which I participate. However, I am not just the passive effect of those worlds, for I actively decide how to interact with them and in so doing I create my concrete empirical self. Also, I am able to recollect, that is, detach myself from the particular self I presently am and evaluate it by comparing it to my being, the self I should be and am called to be; a self which I find deep within me and yet is not my own creation but given to me and imposed on me. Even though I can not spell it out in detail, my being or vocation calls me to open myself and be available to things of nature and to other human beings and to participate in their reality. It calls me to dedicate myself to something or someone beyond my self and my life. In fact, I feel most fully alive, I feel that I *am* most fully, when I orient my life to some cause that transcends it and gives it direction and meaning—even if, in extreme cases, I would have to offer my life for that cause. Who or what is the source of my vocation or ideal self, what a cause such as truth or justice could be that it would call for my total commitment, whether there is something of absolute value at stake in my life, and whether it is possible for us to grasp truths about a sphere beyond the physical are questions that Marcel leaves unanswered here but promises to return to in Volume II. He does suggest, however, that in this life those who commit themselves to a cause beyond themselves can, in their experience of depth, catch glimpses of their fulfillment in a realm beyond time.

COMMENTARY ON VOLUME TWO:

FAITH AND REALITY

I

THE QUESTION OF BEING

Volume II contains the second set of Marcel's Gifford lectures which were given one year after the first. In general he grapples with "questions about the nature of being as such" [II, 1], especially in his first four lectures. This metaphysical or ontological inquiry will move us in a new dimension, he says, yet it will have to fit together with those dimensions of thought contained in Volume I. (As we shall see, he will often make use of analyses and conclusions from last year's lectures and he continues to use the phenomenological method.) He will again employ examples and concrete illustrations to reinforce his arguments, he says, even though he acknowledges that this is much more difficult in metaphysics [II, 2]).

The question about being as such, he goes on, is not a question for thought in general which attempts "to abstract from the inevitably singular experience which is mine"[1] and "think *sub specie aeterni*," that is, by escaping into some alleged timeless and universal "mental stratosphere" [II, 6]. As he has stated repeatedly, that kind of an abstraction from one's human condition is impossible. The inquiry into being must be undertaken by a particular individual's "concrete, personalized thought," prompted by the particular exigencies or demands[2] within that individual [II, 3]. Marcel refers specifically to the exigency for transcendence he discussed in Volume I which he maintained was the impetus behind philosophy. Now he identifies that exigency or demand with the exigency for God which, he states, is "its true face." Accordingly, this year we will deal with questions about being and about God or, more specifically, with faith in God. That will require us to examine the connection between metaphysics and "religious philosophy" and to ask "under what conditions, short of a revelation properly so called, it is possible for us to make affirmations about what God is" [II, 3]. Granted, many famous

---

1   My translation from the French edition, ME, II, 10.

2   As in Volume I, the French word is *exigence*. The translator of this second volume almost always translates it as its English cognate exigency. I will follow him most of the time but occasionally I will use the word demand as I did in the first volume.

metaphysicians of the past have identified being as such with God, but, Marcel insists, only the believer, the living witness to God, "can decide what can or cannot be regarded as God." Therefore, we will have to go more deeply "into what we mean by the believing consciousness" [II, 4].

Before continuing, I would like to make the following observation about Marcel's inquiry into the nature of being as such. Since the word being does not come with some built in or canonical meaning, the important thing for us is to uncover the meanings Marcel himself attaches to the term. Historically, different ontologies devised by different philosophers have used the word being to stand for a variety of things or aspects of things. Although most thinkers have used "being" to refer to very fundamental entities or features of reality, there simply is no one legitimate way, a way which would render all others false, to define that term. Thus, to repeat, we must discover what Marcel himself means.

Since he has stressed that in asking about being we cannot abstract from our concrete existence in the world, Marcel then wonders "how can we give to being a meaning that is intelligible for us?" [II, 5], that is, for all who now and in the future may have contact with his thoughts. In other words, if each person has his or her concrete here and now experience, how can we arrive at common meanings for being, or for anything else for that matter, meanings that can be understood by us all? He answers by claiming that the more I understand my own life and experience, the more "shall I be attuned to an effective understanding of others, of the experiences of others" [II, 7]. That means, he admits, we *can* in some sense philosophize *sub specie aeterni* but, unfortunately, he does not explain exactly what that sense is. May I suggest that he has in mind the fact that we can distinguish between the differing individual here and now features of people's lives and experiences (for example, a particular toothache I feel right now) and those features that are common to every human experience wherever and whenever it exists (toothaches are found everywhere). Insofar as the same common features are present in a multiplicity of differing particular conditions, they can be said to be eternal in the sense that they are not limited to a particular time and place.

Marcel also explains that his recommendation that we attempt to understand our own concrete life experiences does not mean he is advocating ego-centrism for that is obsession with oneself which forms a barrier between me and others. Ego-centrism is even a barrier between me and myself, he states, for if I am separated from, and blind to, the life experiences of others, I am blind to my own as well. Experience confirms that the egoist "is fundamentally in the dark about himself. He does not know his real needs; he does not know what he lacks" [*II, 7-8*].[3] According to last year's analyses, what the self-centered person does not know is that he is deeply tied to others and to his situation; he is not a self-contained or self-sufficient being but vulnerable to other beings which shape and structure him both internally and externally; he is living a narrow, poverty stricken, life for he needs others and needs to share in their lives in order to achieve fulfillment of his own. Egoists are also blind to the fact that "we can understand ourselves by starting from the other, or from others, and only by starting from them" [*II, 8*].

In support of that last statement Marcel states that I can come to love myself only if "I know that I am loved by other beings who are loved by me" [*II, 8*] and in another work he suggests that I become a particular person for myself only through another for whom I am a particular person.[4] That is to say, Marcel believes that I come to know and love my self by the way I am treated and known by others. In support of his position, one could refer to studies in child psychology that have revealed how dependent a person's self-image and self-knowledge are on others. If others regard a child as worthless, evil, and stupid, it is extremely likely that the child, even when he or she becomes an adult, will view him or her self much the same way. And I become aware that I am a lovable person and not just a thing only by encountering other persons or thous who relate to me as a loved person. I believe that is what Marcel is referring to when he writes, "this I seems always to be posited in the face of a thou for whom I am myself a *thou*."[5] In addition, investigations of children raised by animals outside of human society and culture have shown that not only do they not develop into normal human persons, they exhibit the characteristic traits and behaviors of the animals which raised them; absent human contact, they seem to

3   The last phrase in the French edition (ME, II, 11) is omitted in the English translation.

4   MJ, 145.

5   MJ, 146. I have slightly modified the translation from *Journal métaphysique* 145.

consider themselves to be animals. By saying that "we can understand ourselves [only] by starting from the other," he also means, apparently, that I come to know my particular features by first knowing the features of others and then comparing myself to them. Compared to someone well coordinated, I consider myself clumsy; compared to the emotional, I consider myself cool and rational; and so forth.[6]

I would add to these illustrations a general argument that as far as I know Marcel himself does not mention but which seems to follow from the phenomenological perspective he adopts. As we have seen, according to phenomenology, consciousness is first and fundamentally prereflectively conscious of something other than itself and only in a second step does it reflect and become aware of itself. Would it not follow from this that reflective knowledge of the features of one's self is dependent upon one's initial direct awareness of others?

But what does the discussion of one's relation to others have to do with an inquiry into being? Marcel replies by stipulating that the starting point or ground of our inquiry must be "a certain fullness of life" and that such fullness is found only in an intersubjective whole or union of subjects [II, 8-9].[7] Thus, his metaphysics, he says, is not only "a metaphysics of being; it is a metaphysics of *we are* as opposed to a metaphysic of *I think*," [II, 9] like Descartes'.

Can that intersubjective union or nexus, as he now calls it, be expressed clearly in some simple logical proposition, he asks? (I suspect he has in mind the proposition at the basis of Descartes' philosophy: "I think, therefore, I am.") Or, is my experience of the bond "a simple inexpressible intuition," an immediate awareness which cannot be verbalized? Marcel replies that the intersubjective nexus cannot, strictly speaking, be "asserted" like a fact which I am outside of, for I am inside that structure and cannot get outside of it [II, 12]. Likewise, strictly speaking, the intersubjective nexus can not be "given a distinctive designation, that is designated ... [as] 'this' or 'that'; it is not, in fact, *either this or that*. It transcends any disjunction of this kind" [II, 15]. In other words, not only can I not detach myself from it and describe it as an object, I cannot divide the intersubjective bond into separate isolated subjects. It is

---

6   MJ, 146.

7   We shall see in Chapter 3 that one of Marcel's primary meanings for being is the eternal fulness of intersubjective relations.

a *union* of subjects, of whom I am one, who participate in each other and in that way it "transcends" any such disjunction.

Since intersubjective relationships cannot be asserted or designated like objective data, that apparently rules out one of the alternatives mentioned above; the intersubjective nexus can not be asserted in a simple proposition. On the other hand, Marcel grants that intersubjective relations can be acknowledged or recognized and translated into some kind of "expressible affirmations," as he himself is doing and will continue to do, and so our awareness of intersubjectivity is not a totally *inexpressible* intuition either. In fact, he states, an affirmation of the relationship "is the root of every expressible affirmation [and] is the mysterious root of language" *[II, 11]*. (We will return to this shortly.) He also asserts, almost in passing, that although the intersubjective union cannot be given to me as objective data, "it is only this nexus which can allow the thing which is given 'to speak to me'" *[II, 10]*. That is, only because I participate in intersubjective relations do certain things attract my attention *[II, 14]* and have intelligibility and meaning for me. (More also on this shortly.)

One of the difficulties we have in conceiving the intersubjective nexus or structure, Marcel observes, is that for historical reasons we tend to think of ourselves as egos isolated from each other. The truth is rather that the ego is rooted in and emerges from our intersubjective bond or nexus with others *[II, 12]*. We can understand why he says this if we recall that in Volume I, Chapter 9, Marcel described the ego as that part of myself which I focus on because it is exposed and vulnerable to others and which I want others to recognize and approve rather than ignore or harm. Clearly, then, my ego, as he defines it, involves a necessary relation to others and in order for me to construct my ego in the first place I must be aware that there are other *subjects* (that is, other free conscious selves who can know and judge me) before whom I am exposed. That awareness of other subjects, necessary for and prior to my construction of my ego, is, therefore, a subject to subject relation which Marcel claims is rooted in a basic intersubjective bond between us. Indeed, were we insular, self-contained, isolated monads, how could we ever become aware of other subjects? *[II, 18]*. He suggests that the basic intersubjective relationship could be described metaphorically as a spiritual world "in which everything is bound together in ... relations ... [of] living communication" *[II, 15]*. By "living" communication I think he means communication with others that does not involve deliberate, explicit, decisions to communicate. Such communication would be on a prereflective level of experience where we directly nonverbally express our feelings, opinions, values, and so forth, to others, and they to us, without deliberately choosing to do so, without being reflectively aware of doing so, and without knowing exactly how we do so. I advance that interpretation because Marcel also states that the basic intersubjective world "is an implied understanding which remains an implied understanding even when I try to focus my thought on it" [II, 15]. The phrase "implied understanding" is, I submit, what elsewhere he has called, more technically, prereflective or nonreflective consciousness or intuition, meaning a direct immediate awareness of something, in this case of other subjects and our bond with them. Such an intuition, he is saying, remains present even when it is reflected upon or focused on and reflection on it can never bring it fully to explicit awareness. That intersubjective world and our prereflective consciousness of it is also referred to at the end of this chapter when he speaks of my *"more or less distinct consciousness of the underlying unity which ties me to other beings [subjects] of whose reality I already have a preliminary feeling"* and of "the presence of an underlying reality that is felt, of a community which is deeply rooted in ontology" [II, 17].[8] "Without this [community] human relations in any real sense would be unintelligible," he says.

Let me try and put all this together. Marcel holds that there is an underlying *felt* intersubjective nexus or community, a bond of living communication between subjects, that is present on the prereflective or intuitive level of experience.[9] Our nonreflective felt awareness of that underlying intersubjective community is, he claims, at the basis of all subsequent human relations and at the root of language, and it also explains why some things attract our attention and possess intelligibility and meaning for us. In support of his position, he argues that it is only because we are prereflectively aware of others *as subjects* (not objects or things), that we can choose to enter into further intersubjective relations and communicate with them. As he says in a later work, that awareness of others as subjects is a "basic experience" which provides "existential assurance" that human beings are open to each other and can and do

---

8   My translation from ME, II, 20.

9   In last year's terminology, that underlying intersubjective unity with others is a type of submerged participation.

communicate.[10] I can choose to join others in human relations of friendship, fidelity and love, for example, only because, whether I ever explicitly formulate it or not, I am first aware of others as subjects. Also, to use language to communicate with others presupposes that I am, at least implicitly, aware and assured that other subjects exist with experiences similar to mine who can, therefore, understand and respond to me. No doubt it is through my experience of the speech and behavior of other subjects that I learn language in the first place and that through it my attention is directed to specific things and features of reality which, also through language, acquire significance and meaning for me *[II, 12-14]*. (A couple of examples: the Eskimo language has hundreds of words for the numerous varieties of snow and one of the native languages of the Philippines, Tagalog, has numerous words to designate the many variations of green. Children inheriting those languages become far more aware of specific types of snow and their significance and specific types of green and their significance than do English speakers who can add only a few adjectives to the nouns in question.)

Marcel concludes his initial foray into the question of being by asking, "Can we say that being *is* intersubjectivity?" His guarded response is no, if "this proposition ... is taken literally," yet he concedes that a thought directed toward being "recreates around itself the intersubjective presence" *[II, 16]*. Or, to put it another way, "the more the *ego* realizes it is but one among others, among an infinity of others with whom it maintains relations," the more it feels "the density of being" *[II, 16-17]*. Whatever characteristics we eventually assign to being as such, he declares, I concern myself with being only insofar as I am conscious of my unity with other beings or subjects who are my fellow-travelers and fellow-creatures *[II, 17]*. Thus, even if being is not literally intersubjectivity for Marcel, the two are certainly intimately connected. Finally, may I point out that in this chapter he has begun to refer to subjects as "beings." For now the term seems to be equivalent to the term subject but later we shall see that it has a much richer meaning.

Pages in other works of Marcel that treat material of this chapter:
TW, 39-41.   CF, 33-36, 56, 68-70.   MJ, 145-47.

---

10 TW, 39-41.

2

EXISTENCE AND BEING

Marcel continues his ontological investigation in this lecture and devotes a lot of time to discussing the difference, if any, between being and existence. In the light of what comes later, let me make two initial comments. In the first place, most of his analyses of being and existence are suspended toward the end of the chapter because they are a "rather barren field of speculation" [II, 30]. Secondly, it is only in *Tragic Wisdom and Beyond*, published over twenty years after *The Mystery of Being*, that Marcel clearly recognizes and sets forth the *three* different meanings the term being has in his thought.[1] Therefore, I will use some of *Tragic Wisdom...* in my commentary here and in later chapters since it will help clarify many of the different things he says about being.

Marcel begins by pointing out that in both English and French the term being (*être*) is deeply ambiguous [II, 18-19]. It can be taken as a substantive or noun as when I ask, What is the entity (*étant*) called being? Or, being can be a verb as when I ask "what does to be (i.e. the fact of being) mean?" To ask what is being as such, then, can be to ask "what does *to be* [a verb] mean or again what is it that makes a being to be a *being* [a noun]?" [II, 19].

In the first place, Marcel observes, citing Aristotle, being is not an ordinary property of something but is a transcendental for it is "what makes possible the existence of any property at all" [II ,20]. Being is not one property among others, like color, size or density, for being applies to or infuses each and every property; in order for color, size or density to exist they must *be*. Any entity, any part or feature of any entity must be in order to exist. Yet being is also not prior to all properties or entities as if in itself it lacked all qualifications. To call being a transcendental is to declare that it is not limited to just one category but includes them all—for again, everything that exists or is must possess being, or, more simply, must be.

---

1   In TW, Chapter 4, the three meanings are: 1. Being as foundation—which he will discuss in this chapter; 2. Being as fullness—which he will discuss in Chapters 3 and 10; 3. Being when said of *a* being—which he discusses in many places but especially in Chapters 4 and 5.

Marcel then goes on to spell out just what he means by the transcendental being. He states that there is "a most intimate connection between being pure and simply ... and the being of the copula, the verb of [the] judgment of predication," namely the verb "is" in S is P *[II, 20].*[2] To assign attributes to something, for example, to say the sea is green, is, he says, to stress certain specific features of the more comprehensive and basic affirmation, the sea *is.* Of course, I seldom bother to make a simple affirmation of something's being; most often it happens when a new being such as a baby makes its appearance in the world *[II, 21].*[3] To speak of the appearance of something in the world, however, reminds him of the meaning he gave in volume I to the term existence, namely, the sensible appearance of things, and the rest of this chapter consists of a discussion "of the relation between being and existence" *[II, 22].*

Before following him into that discussion, I want to highlight the meaning Marcel has given to being in the pages just covered. He has identified being with the copula of a proposition, the is of S is P; to assert the being of something is to state that it *is.* "We are involved in being" he writes in *Being and Having,* "more simply we are."[4] In addition, since being is a transcendental which includes all that is, he also refers to it as "plenary reality,"[5] "omnipresent,"[6] and "inexhaustible."[7]

Now being in this sense, the "is" of whatever is, being "taken as a verb rather than a noun," is called being as foundation in the later work *Tragic Wisdom* ....[8] It is the foundation of all particular beings, Marcel states, since "the fact or act of being [the is of whatever is] comes first relative to any possible specifications."[9] It is so fundamental that "strictly speaking" it cannot be questioned "since every question presupposes

---

2   In his earlier *Being and Having* he made the same point: "we must attach the 'being' of the copula to being simply." BH, 122.

3   The affirmation "God is" is a special case, he says, which he will examine later. The translator incorrectly translates *être* (ME, II, 24-25) as existence on (II, 21-23).

4   BH, 35.

5   Ibid.

6   BH, 36.

7   CF, 69.

8   TW, 51, 53, 59.

9   TW, 49.

being as a base;"[10] that is, without being in this sense I who question "am not" and "indeed, nothing is."[11] Since the fact or act of being is prior (ontologically, not temporally) to all possible determinations of it, it is "at a level beneath the world of things, the world of 'such and such' ... beneath any determinate 'thisness.' We are at the level of what might be called thisness in general, or the level of the foundation grounding any 'this.'"[12] In like manner, being as foundation transcends the opposition between subject and object and underlies them—for both are. Even though it is beneath all determinations, it is not, however, an empty abstraction for as the foundation of all beings, it "is the fundamental and indissoluble bond" between them and "the unity which enwraps" them all,[13] for, again, as a transcendental it includes all that is. In early works Marcel sometimes uses the language of participation when speaking of the relation between beings and being as foundation. "To say 'A is, B is, etc.,' he writes, " seems to me equivalent to saying 'A participates in being, B participates in being, etc.'"[14] and, accordingly, he claims that "a blindfold knowledge of being in general is implied in all particular knowledge" of particular beings.[15] (Being in general is what he later calls being as foundation.) The blindfold, implicit knowledge of being present in our explicit awareness of particular beings is subsequently designated as a prereflective (hence, blindfold) consciousness or an intuition of being.[16] In some works he refers to that implicit knowledge of being as a fundamental "assurance .... which we cannot do without."[17] Of course we cannot do without it because, as he says, it "underlies the development of all thought,"[18] and of everything else, for it is the foundational assurance that we and everything that is participate in being. In other words, that we *are*.[19]

---

10   Ibid.

11   TW, 52.

12   TW, 51.

13   TW, 51; BH, 29.

14   BH, 35. See also CF, 56.

15   BH, 28.

16   MAMS, 228.

17   TW, 62, CA, 183.

18   CA, 183.

19   TW, 50-53.

Let us return now to Marcel's discussion in *The Mystery* ... of the relation between being and existence. His first step is to address the position of St. Thomas Aquinas as related by the twentieth century Thomist and historian of philosophy, Etienne Gilson. Aquinas categorically identifies existence (*esse* in Latin) with being *[II, 22]*.[20] That prompts him to revisit last year's discussion of existence.[21] As he did then, he quotes from the appendix of his early *Metaphysical Journal* where he writes that existence is either "the sensible presence of the thing [or] its manifestation, its most immediate revelation" *[II, 23]*. Now, he says, he is not willing to distinguish the "sensible presence" of the thing and its "manifestation" *[II, 24]*, which is to say that existence *is* the sensible presence of a thing. Of course, that limits the application of the term to mutable sensible things, as he in fact did in last year's lectures. However, he admits here that it is not that simple because he recognizes that we often speak of the existence of entities that are not just things. For example, my own body "is at the same time a thing and yet in some way more than a thing" *[II, 25]*. The human body can be treated like a thing yet to treat a human being only as a thing (for example by enslaving or torturing him or her) is inhuman precisely because a human is more than a thing. He or she is also a subject, a living "center" of conscious acts which is aware of itself and its inner life ("interiority") and of its ability to determine its own life. (Later he will explicitly say what he seems to imply here, namely, that to be a subject is to possess value.) The question, then, becomes what do the words "to cease to exist" mean when applied to a human subject? No doubt, if one considers Napoleon just a thing or bodily mechanism, that mechanism no longer exists. However, as we saw in last year's lectures, a person's body cannot be reduced to a thing-like mechanism; it is a "presence" because that person, that subject, *is* his or her body. And, Marcel contends, if we do not reduce the dead to a bodily mechanism "it is extremely doubtful whether to say 'they no longer exist' has any meaning at all" *[II, 26]*.

That shows, he states, "that the idea of existence ... is fundamentally involved in an ambiguity" *[II, 26]*. "The existence of a thing regarded only as a thing" is certainly "under the shadow of the threat of ceasing

---

20 After his conversion to Roman Catholicism, Marcel was instructed in Thomism by the leading twentieth century neo-Thomist, Jacques Maritian. See *Awakenings*, 126-27 and EBHD, 81.

21 Volume I, Chapter 3.

not diminish but enhances those involved.[1] As for pantheism, it is a "crude materialism," he states, that thinks of God "only as an idol and not as a spirit" *[II, 35]*. I assume he identifies pantheism with materialism because the latter believes that the intersubjective union of entities results in the obliteration of at least one of them; but that is true only of material unions (as when I eat an apple) not of spiritual unions (as when I know or love another). Furthermore, pantheism's "depersonalized conception of being," namely, of God, is only an idol compared to his own conception of God as a supremely personal absolute Thou.

Returning to his discussion of the relation between existence and being, Marcel wonders whether we have "been rash in leaving our inquiry into *being in general* in order to examine what it is I envisage when I speak of *my being?*" *[II, 36]*, for while questions about being in general are about "everything which is," questions about my being are obviously much narrower. He responds that the objection, insofar as it refers to being in general, rests on the presumption that being "is something like a predicate" that can be "ascribed to anything at all," that is, to all the "things which are" *[II, 36]*.[2] "That road leads nowhere," he states. I presume he has in mind his analysis in the previous chapter where he maintained that being was not one predicate among others nor, strictly speaking, a predicate at all because being makes all predicates be in the first place. Also, he said there that being should be understood in terms of the copula "is" in S is P, not in terms of the predicate, P. Yet, if we go the opposite route and try and treat being as a contentless subject in relation to all possible predicates, that too is incorrect, he maintains, because being is a transcendental which includes *all* that is *[II, 20-21]*. It follows that we cannot conceive of being in the "categories of traditional logic," he concludes. Let me point out, however, that "traditional" Aristotelian logic which recognized the transcendentals also held that, as a transcendental, being can be predicated of all that is, even if, strictly speaking, it cannot be designated as a predicate which belongs in a particular logical category. In fact, as we pointed out earlier, being, meaning the fact or act of being, the "is" of whatever is, is what Marcel himself later calls being as foundation in which all that is participates. Now he simply dismisses that notion of being because, he states, to investigate

---

1   Volume I, Chapter 9.

2   My translation from the French, ME, II, 38. Again, the translator renders a form of *être* as existence.

it would lead us "to betray the exigence for being" and, he adds, "it is to obtaining a more and more precise consciousness of this that our efforts are directed" [II. 37]. That statement comes as something of a surprise since nowhere in the previous two chapters did he say that he was primarily concerned with being insofar as it fulfills our exigency or demand for being. Be that as it may, he proceeds to investigate our exigency for being and the nature of the being which would fulfill it. (Note by the way, that he has now identified the exigency for transcendence, first mentioned in Chapter 3 of Volume I, not only with the exigency for God, in Chapter 1 of this volume, but also with the exigency for being.)

The exigency for being, he asserts, is not a "simple desire or a vague aspiration" but "a deep-rooted inner urge" [II, 37]. Nor is it a need or want; it is an inner *demand* for being.[3] To make this clearer he returns to his critique of our over functionalized world in which there is "a weakening of the sense of being" [II, 38] and a debasement of human relations. As we saw last year in his discussion of the broken world, Marcel objects to the reduction of the individual to his or her functions, that is, to the social role he or she plays in some larger organization. Such a restriction denies people the freedom and creativity to transcend their functions and it degrades human relationships into a mere meeting of functions. Furthermore, in our complicated world with its extreme division of labor, functions have become so fragmented and diminished that they have lost both their value and interest. Think, for example, of a person on an assembly line repeating the same minimal activity hour after hour or a clerk in a high tech office who enters data into a computer all day every day. What value can such reduced functions have for them? Some people acutely feel the emptiness of such a world and that is because, he says, they feel the ontological exigency, the deep inner urge or demand for being. Still, is that felt exigency anything more than a sentimental nostalgia for a less technological era, he asks, that has no "real metaphysical significance;" in other words, is the exigency a purely subjective feeling which reveals nothing about reality [II, 40]?

If I understand it correctly, Marcel's basic response to that question is that feelings are not purely subjective phenomena for they have objects. However, he argues his position by referring to an obscure passage

---

3   On (II, 37) Marcel criticizes an early translation of CA. I pass over his remarks since I am using a later and much better translation.

from the American philosopher William Ernest Hocking[4] which he interprets as denying an opposition between our faculty of knowing and our faculty of feeling. (Such an opposition would occur when feeling is considered to be a purely subjective internal unconscious state while knowing is regarded as grasping real external objects but to totally lack feeling.) Whatever else it says, the quotation from Hocking appears to maintain that all positive feelings are not unconscious, purely subjective, phenomena but are cognitive experiences or experimental knowledge of what he calls ideas embodied in objects—whose embodiment is due to feeling *[II, 41]*. Rather than further analyze Hocking's remarks, may I suggest that we can make Marcel's point more simply by pointing out that in the phenomenological tradition which he accepts, feelings are considered to be conscious acts and since, as Husserl said, all consciousness is consciousness of something, feelings are not purely internal states but are intentional, that is, feelings have objects—which in Hocking's terminology would be ideas embodied in objects.

Still, Marcel goes on, one can ask if those embodied ideas are true ideas, which I interpret to be much the same question he posed earlier, namely, is the urgent felt exigency for being directed toward something true or real or is it purely subjective? That question, he asserts without explanation, makes us face "the notion of value" *[II, 41]* and he returns to his criticisms of our overfunctionalized world and points out that one can critique it only "by the standard of certain values." (He notes in passing that those cynics who mock critiques of our present world as too idealistic and who advocate instead a "realistic" facing of the facts are themselves invoking values and attributing them to the status quo which they assume is permanent *[II, 43]*.) Now the question persists in a slightly different form, are the values used to critique our society anything more than subjective preferences of likes and dislikes? That asks, of course, about the true character of values and it prompts Marcel to assert that we have "a vague assurance that being can only be nominally distinct from a certain fullness of truth" *[II, 42]*— a statement that needs some explanation.

---

4   Hocking (1873-1966) had a long teaching career at Harvard University. He was in the classical idealist tradition and drew heavily on mystical experience of God. His major work is considered to be his first of ten books, *The Meaning of God in Human Experience*, which Marcel cites. I might note that he gave the Gifford lectures in 1938-39 a few years before Marcel.

Being involves "a certain fullness" for Marcel because it is on the basis of our exigency for being that we criticize "the hollowness of a functionalized world" where human beings are reduced to members of a species (specimens)[II, 42] rather than being considered as unique individuals each possessing inherent dignity and value. Being must be, then, a fullness by comparison to which our world appears empty and, as he said last year, broken—because it renders intimate human relationships increasingly difficult. What Marcel means by being as fullness must, therefore, include intimate intersubjective relationships which respect the intrinsic dignity of every human being.

But why does he maintain that being is also a fullness of *truth?* The reason becomes clear if we recall that what in this volume he designates as an exigency for being, in Volume I he described as an intellectual exigency for transcendence, and by transcendence he meant a purer and fuller mode of experience filled with intelligibility and truth [I, 55-56]. Thus, as Marcel looks at it, our deep inner urge or exigency for being is for both a fullness of intersubjective relations and of truth.

In order to clarify even more the nature of the fullness he has in mind, Marcel addresses throughout the chapter a number of things he does not mean by it and I will group them together here. First, fullness when said of being "must not be understood quantitatively as ... the total of a sum" [II, 42] or as a whole or totality made up of homogeneous units added together [II, 50]. Second, being as fullness is not something that should be considered in itself, rather it is "something to satisfy a profound requirement" [II, 45], namely our inner demand for being. Third, being as fulfillment is not a phase in a development of growth and dissolution for as fullness or plenitude, being can not decline. On the other hand, fourth, fullness does not mean perfection like "a work which has taken on its final and definitive form" [II, 47] nor does it mean that which is complete in and of itself or self-sufficient like "a whole closed in on itself " [II, 48-49]. Finally, by being as fullness Marcel does not mean "a universal being" or highest genus reached through "abstract denominations" [II, 50], for the most abstract is the most lacking in content.

Fullness or fulfillment "can take on a positive meaning," he states, "only from the point of view of creation" [II, 45], not necessarily the creation of an external product but, for example, the creation of a spiritual community of love and of "the invisible work which gives the human adventure the only meaning which can justify it"—I presume he means the concrete creation of values such as peace, beauty, justice, and truth.

Fulfillment, also, "should be interpreted ... as a mode of participation in" the spiritual realm of intersubjectivity [II, 46] and he offers a concrete illustration. "An experience of fulness," he states, is "like that which is involved in love, when love ... experiences itself as shared" [II, 49].[5] Being as fullness, then, for Marcel involves the creation of and conscious participation in an intersubjective union or community of lovers who experience their shared love and common union, a community that also seeks to create and participate in peace, beauty, justice and other works that give meaning to human life. Needless to say, such a union is not a quantitative sum of human beings added together, any more than a musical chord or melody is just a sum of notes which compose it [II, 50]. Nor is it something perfect or complete for, as we saw in volume I, an intersubjective union is not static but a living community of persons united in a vital, creative, fructifying milieu.[6] Nor is it an empty universal genus but "a type of unity which holds together a number of persons within a life which they share."[7] Finally, since being also includes a certain fullness of truth, the intersubjectivity he has in mind must be a community of persons advancing both "in love and in truth" [II, 183]. Thus for Marcel being as fullness is a loving community composed of those animated by a love of truth and of other human values who delight in being with each other in building that community.

As so described, being as fullness, he insists, is not simply a datum as a fact or object that just is in itself [II, 44]; it is rather, he repeats, that which fulfills a deep need within us, our ontological exigency or demand, and, as such, that being is the fundamental value that we seek. Still, is that value that we so deeply desire "only an ideal... regarded as something more or less nebulous," he wonders, "only the aspiration of an incurably romantic sentimentality?" [II, 42-43]. That has been his recurring question: is being as fullness real or is it only a purely subjective and nebulous ideal? Of course, his answer is to appeal to experience. "There is an experience of being," he argues, and "the experience of being, it is fulfillment" [II, 44].[8] We were given his illustrations of

---

5   He distinguishes between the unconscious fulfillment realized in natural things, such as the flower or fruit of a plant, from the fulfillment that is aware of itself in human beings [II, 46].

6   CF, 35.

7   HV, 155.

8   I have slightly modified the translation, ME, II, 46.

fulfillment earlier. One spoke of the creation of charity and love in human life and of all that gives life meaning and value *[II, 45]*. The other was more concrete: "an experience of fulness," he said, is "like that which is involved in love, when love ... experiences itself as shared" *[II, 49]*. It appears that Marcel is saying that we experience being as fullness to some degree when we experience shared love and, more generally, when we participate in a community of lovers who seek those things that give life meaning and value. In other words, our deep inner urge for being as fullness is neither for some pie in the sky ideal nor for a return of the past; it is for a multifaced but concrete reality that we already have experienced to some degree. Needless to say, in this life we have not and cannot attain or, better, participate completely in being as fullness for we never experience love or truth or justice or beauty in their plenitude. That plenitude he calls *"being par excellence"* at the end of this chapter *[II, 51]* and in *Tragic Wisdom* ... says it "is most genuinely being."[9] Naturally that raises the question whether experience offers us any indication that we can or will ever attain *being par excellence?* We shall see later that Marcel answers yes to this question.

He concludes this chapter by wondering whether by denying that being is perfection or totality or an object or something to which predicates could be ascribed, he has rendered it so insubstantial that we cannot "legitimately speak of it at all?" *[II, 51]*. The question is perplexing given his description of being as a living union of subjects aware of being bound together in love and of searching for truth and for other values that make life meaningful. Why is he worried that such a community may be too insubstantial? In any case, he will pursue that concern in the next chapter, although he will eventually realize that any question about the "substantification" of being is misguided.

There is one other item I should mention. Since Marcel has identified the exigency for being with the exigency for God, it is strange that God is not referred to in his description of being as fullness and, especially, of *being par excellence*. Actually, God is an essential part of being as fullness but only at the end of these lectures will Marcel indicate the connection between them.

Pages in other works of Marcel that treat material of this chapter:
TW, 50-53, 223-29.   CA, 172-76   EBHD, 76-78.

---

9   TW, 53.

4
THE LEGIMITACY OF ONTOLOGY

his is a perplexing chapter. After spending over half of it engaging
in a technical discussion about the legitimacy of "substantifying"
being, Marcel suddenly realizes that the notion of substantification itself is "faulty" [II, 60]. Still, even in those pages in the first portion
of the chapter he makes important statements about the meaning of
being especially when said of *a* being. In fact, his primary concern in
the chapter is the meaning of the term being when it is predicated of
individual human beings.

   He initiates his discussion by observing that the question, is it legitimate
to substantify being, presupposes we have a standard to which something
must conform in order to be legitimate, but where would we obtain such
a standard, he asks? "What we need is something which will provide
a starting point from which we may arrive at some standards" [II, 52].
Now the starting point, "the basis of all our affirmations," must, of course,
be "experience itself, treated as a massive presence [that is]... looked at
in the indivisibility of its different aspects" [II, 53]. He highlights the
word "indivisible" and explains that he "is opposed to all specification
... which is isolated from other specifications." Experience is a massive
amalgamation of all kinds of different features and we must not reduce
it to only one of them—for example, by trying to explain all human
affairs in economic or sociological or biological categories. Nor should
we isolate features one from another as if they have no connection or
influence on each other.

   The reality we are looking for, he says, is both "infinitely distant" and
"quite near" and only by accepting that paradox can we "hope to reach
an understanding of faith" [II, 53-54]. As we know, the reality we are
looking for is being but why he claims it is both distant and near, and
what it has to do with faith, is not explained at this time. Instead, he
proceeds to list four hypotheses about the substantification or nonsub-
stantification of particular beings and of *being par excellence* which he
now also refers to as being in itself. Before presenting that list, however,
let me remark that what exactly Marcel means by the terms substantify
or substantification is sometimes not very clear. Strictly speaking, to
substantify something is to make it substance-like and occasionally

he does appear to mean by substantify to consider something to be an object or a thing, something expressed as a noun. Yet, other times, and more frequently, he apparently means by substantify to consider something to possess value.

In any case the following are his four hypotheses:[1]

1. Is it legitimate to substantify individual beings but not being in itself?
2. Is it illegitimate to substantify both?
3. Is it legitimate to substantify being in itself but not particular beings?
4. Is it legitimate to substantify both as we do in ordinary language? *[II, 54]*

Now if we refuse to treat a "particular being as being,"[2] (which I presume means to refuse to substantify it) we reduce human beings to functions or numbers, Marcel explains, and that is to not treat them as subjects and involves "real suppression of the value of [their] being" *[II, 55]*. It also makes human relations less than human because they are not genuinely intersubjective. Granted, we can consider humans as objects which may be described and counted but that is to view them only as material things. "We acknowledge them as beings," he explains, "when they become for us, in some degree, centers or focal points" *[II, 57]*. Earlier we saw that he referred to subjects as "centers" because they have "interiority," a life of their own *[II, 25]* . Thus, when we consider human persons as centers we see them as unique agents who are aware of themselves as conscious and free sources of their physical and mental activities. They live "their own" lives since they themselves consciously choose their goals and behavior and are aware of doing so. To consider human beings as centers or focal points is also to consider them as having value, as he said above. Now as valuable centers or subjects, they can "evoke in us a reaction of love and respect or a contrary reaction of fear or even horror" *[II, 57]*— although the latter reaction, he admits, involves a contradiction, perhaps because it is to react negatively to something of value. Because they provoke such feelings in us, "it is not quite possible to de-substantify individual beings" *[II, 56]*, Marcel claims, which in the context means it is not quite possible to consider human beings as objects or things which possess no inherent value.

But is it possible, he goes on, to "admit that there are *individual beings* and at the same time [claim] that *being* is not?" *[II, 56]*.[3] (The first

1   For some reason the translator condenses them into three. See Marcel's list, ME, II, 55.
2   My translation from the French, ME, II, 56.
3   My translation from the French, ME, II, 57.

hypothesis.) Putting this in terms of substantification, if we substantify individual beings can we refuse "to substantify being"? *[II, 57]*.[4] To deny substantification of being as such by asserting that "nothing is" is "radical metaphysical nihilism," according to Marcel. To claim that nothing is does not mean literally that there is nothing that exists or is real but rather that "nothing resists, or could resist, the test of critical experience" *[II, 58]*. That means, he explains elsewhere, there is nothing of inherent value, no being, that "would withstand an exhaustive analysis of the data of experience that would try to reduce them progressively to elements that are increasingly devoid of any intrinsic value or significance."[5] In other words, to maintain that "nothing is" is to claim that in the final analysis nothing in our experience possesses real value. Needless to say that position has clear repercussions on our idea of individual beings, for to believe that "no being is," that is, that nothing has intrinsic value means, of course, "there are no individual beings" *[II, 58]*, that is, no individual things have inherent value. (The second hypothesis.) And, Marcel suggests, it is because all "individual beings are liable to decay" that some generalize and conclude that "being is not,"[6] that is, "there is nothing of which it can be asserted that it is indestructible or eternal" *[II, 59]*. Note that this means that for Marcel, what has intrinsic value, and so can resist the reduction of experience to meaningless elements, must be indestructible or eternal. Any value that could cease to be is in the long run one that can not withstand that reduction.

Yet can it be legitimate, he asks, to assert "the non-reality of individual beings?", that is, to hold that they are simply ephemeral appearances on the surface of a reality which is substantial, namely, being in itself? *[II, 59]*. (The third hypothesis.) He suggests that there may actually be only a "nominal distinction between the two," meaning that what can be treated as being in one case can be qualified as nonbeing in another, and he points out that historically many mystics and philosophers have done so *[II, 60]*. However, he thinks that this happens because they have not expressed the problem of being precisely or clearly enough and to avoid that confusion he returns to some of the things he said in Chapter 2 about being as it is experienced in love. "When we are dealing with an individual being, apprehended in its quality of being—*that is to say loved* ... then the meaning of the word 'perish' is by no means clear," he states,

---

4   My translation from the French, ME, II, 59,

5   CA. 175.

6   My translation from the French, ME, II, 60.

because perish is a physical process which can be described objectively. However, since "ontology is bound up with intersubjectivity, then those processes can find no place in the ontological order," the order of being [II, 60]. In other words, when we are dealing with subjects or beings joined in love, physical processes do not apply.

That leads him to recognize that the four hypotheses he set forth earlier, affirming or denying the substantification of individual beings and/or being itself, are faulty in their formulation for the expressions substantify or substantification imply we are thinking of being as a thing or object, even a physical object like a "compact, massive block ... one could call being in itself" [II, 60-61]. However, being is not an object which is in itself, he repeats, for "being cannot be separated from the exigency for being" which is "the fundamental reason for the impossibility of severing being from value" [II, 61].[7] As he insisted in the previous chapter, the exigency for being is not for some brute object but for that which is intrinsically valuable and, as he stated earlier in this chapter, to experience another as a being is to experience him or her as inherently of value. Furthermore, since he has argued that being's value is imperishable or eternal, that means that the exigency for being and the exigency for perennialness are inseparable. To illustrate, Marcel again refers to the experience of love which is the experience of the beloved as a being and at the same time the experience that he or she "shall not die." The affirmation of the beloved as a being, as possessing intrinsic value, involves the recognition that "there is something in thou[8] which can bridge the abyss that I vaguely call 'death'" [II, 62] and that "something," Marcel says, is the "substantial value" *of the beloved*. That means, he insists, that love is not just an internal subjective feeling but "is the active refusal to treat itself as subjective," which is to say that love believes that the beloved will not die because it experiences something *real* in the beloved, namely, that he or she is a being, he or she possesses eternal value. And love's refusal to treat itself as subjective "cannot be separated from faith," he asserts, "in fact it is faith" [II, 62].

Of course, strictly rational thought will say that such a refusal involves "a monstrous claim [which is] a violation of the very conditions

---

7   Actually, most of the times substantify is used in this chapter it has meant to cause or consider something to be of value. Also, in spite of the reservations he has just expressed, he will continue to speak of substantification in connection with ontology (*II, 62*).

8   The French word is *toi* not *vous*, ME, II, 62.

of experience,"[9] namely, the conditions that everything that exists is doomed to deterioration and to perishing. But that criticism comes from the perspective of primary refection, Marcel counters, and we must transcend it by using secondary reflection to investigate faith, the faith present in love *[II, 62, 67].*[10] (That means, he explains below, that we must investigate faith by sympathetically joining in the believer's experience, not by viewing it and the believer from the outside as objects.)

To provide a concrete illustration of the relations between reflection and faith, Marcel summarizes his play *Castles of Sand*. I will not repeat his review except to say that the play portrays the effect of primary or critical reflection on the faith of two characters. That reflection claims that "to believe means to imagine that" something is the case, namely, that God is. "Fundamentally," he says, "this criticism acts by reduction" *[II, 67]*, which might be something like the following. I imagine that there is a God because of my infantile desire for a father to protect and reward me (a psychological reduction), or because faith is part of my identity as someone of Irish heritage (a sociological reduction). But primary reflection's reductive explanations of faith are from the outside, Marcel maintains, "that is from the moment when we cease to live it" *[II, 66]*. Secondary reflection will investigate faith from the inside, as it is lived and experienced by the believer, and from that vantage point will critique the reductive approach of primary reflection. In doing so, secondary reflection "while not yet being itself faith, succeeds," he says, "in preparing or fostering what I am ready to call the spiritual setting of faith" *[II, 66]*, presumably by removing misunderstandings of it and revealing its true character in human experience. That is his task in the next chapter.

Passages in other works of Marcel that treat material of this chapter:
TW, 47-55.   CA, 175-76.
MJ, 62-63, 179-84, 303-04.

---

9   I have slightly modified the translation from the French, ME, II, 63.

10   The translation *(II, 62)* reads "hidden affinities between secondary reflection and thought." However the French word is *foi* not *pensée*, ME, II, 62.

5
OPINION AND FAITH

Marcel begins his reflections on faith by summarizing his treatment of opinion and faith found in some of his earlier works.[1] As he describes it, "one can have an opinion only of that of which one has no knowledge ... but ... this lack of knowledge is not self-evident or self-admitted" [II, 64]. Furthermore, opinion wavers between a pure impression (my impression is or it seems that Bill is honest) and an affirmation (Bill is honest), and he states that "opinion properly so called seems always to imply" the latter, "a *I maintain that*" Bill is honest [II, 69]. Since to maintain is to claim, Marcel defines an opinion as "a *seeming which tends to become a claiming*" [II, 70] because of a lack of reflection. In many cases a person is so "*submerged* by his surroundings" [II, 71] that his or her opinions simply reflect those of others, the press, the anonymous "they" or "everyone."[2]

Marcel goes on to make a very important distinction within opinion between its pure and impure elements. The pure or ideal element consists of a "more or less articulate affirmation of certain values" (for example, justice and equality) [II, 71] while the impure element consists in a claim that is not reflected on. Elsewhere he gives a helpful illustration of what he means.[3] In speaking to an audience of communists, he realized that they, like he, affirmed genuine values such as justice and equality—the pure elements in their opinion. However, they also maintained that they knew, or "everyone knew," who was responsible for the injustices and inequalities in society, namely the wealthy capitalists or ruling class; that was the impure element.

Next he applies his analysis to opinions in religious matters, especially those of the militant atheist who *maintains* that God does not exist [II, 72]. Of course, the atheist has no direct experience which confirms his or her belief, at best he or she simply has no experience of God's reality. More often, atheists point to the presence of evil in the world and claim that it is incompatible with the existence of a God "who is

---

1 Especially CF, Chapter 6.

2 CF, 124-25.

3 CF, 125-26.

both completely good and completely powerful" [II, 73]. The notion that God is all good and powerful, along with the factual existence of evil, "might well be granted," Marcel observes; they would be the pure elements in the atheists' opinion. But we need not accept the impure elements, the alleged incompatibility between such a God and evil. On what basis can atheists make that claim, for they cannot put themselves in God's place to judge his behavior. Furthermore, if we recognize that "the affirmation of God cannot be separated from the existence of free beings" [II, 74] whom he has created, then we may have to admit that God must permit human beings to exercise their freedom even when they choose to do evil. He grants that such a solution to the existence of evil is not "metaphysically satisfactory" [II, 75], presumably because there is much evil in the world not caused by human freedom. He also suggests that the traditional distinction between what God permits (for example, evil caused by human freedom) and what God wills (for example, the well being of all) is relevant. Rather than pursue this any further at this time, he returns to the distinction between opinion and faith by investigating conviction which, he says, is "midway between the two." Conviction also seems to be part of faith or belief.

As Marcel describes it, conviction, that is "the fact of *being convinced that*" [II, 75], consists of taking a definite position about something. The person who is convinced "claims the assurance that nothing which may happen later will modify his way of thinking" [II, 75], or, as he puts it in another work, conviction, because it is unchangeable "embodies a claim to arrest time."[4] Now the believer may look like someone who is convinced that God exists but, Marcel insists, belief and conviction involve "two completely different vistas" [II, 78] or perspectives. He characterizes conviction as closed. "It implies a kind of inner closure"[5] he writes, for it states that "whatever happens or whatever may be said cannot alter what I think."[6] Faith, on the other hand, is open [II, 86] for it involves *believing in* something or someone, not *believing that* (or being convinced that) a certain creed or set of propositions are true. That is, faith consists of placing oneself "at the disposal of something" [II, 77], of "*giving oneself to, rallying to;*"[7] it involves "an existential index," namely,

---

4 CF, 131.

5 CF, 133.

6 CF, 131.

7 CF, 134.

a person's concrete here and now pledge to give oneself to and "to follow" something or someone. Since belief gives one's self, "the strongest belief, or more exactly, the most living belief, is that which absorbs most fully all the powers of your being" *[II, 78]*. For its part, conviction does not involve a pledge of one's self or a giving of one's self or a commitment to follow anything; it simply pronounces an unchangeable judgment about something.

Now what is it that one pledges to or commits one's self to or rallies to, that is, what does one believe in, Marcel asks and he answers, "it is always a reality, whether personal or suprapersonal." (Elsewhere, he indicates that by suprapersonal he means causes such as justice, peace, freedom.)[8] In other words, faith is always in something or someone that "presents itself to me as incapable of being reduced to the condition which is that of *things*" *[II, 79]* for things can never respond to me. "To believe in someone," he says, "is to place confidence in him, is to say: 'I am sure that thou will not betray my expectation, that thou will respond to it, that thou will fulfill it'" *[II, 79]*.[9] Marcel himself calls attention to his use of the familiar form of you here, which, as we saw last year, refers to another as a person in intimate loving union with me. Only a thou can be invoked, he states, and can become "something to which one can have recourse" for only a thou, a person in loving union with me, can give me the confidence that my expectations will not be betrayed but responded to. What expectations is he talking about? In other works he indicates that one expectation is that I will receive assistance to enable me to remain faithful to my pledge come what may.[10] I recognize that I am weak and cannot count on my own resources to maintain my faith, especially when faced with serious temptations to betray it. Faith in a thou, then, contains the confidence and expectation that the thou will offer me the assistance I need to keep my pledge no matter what happens. In addition, I believe for Marcel faith also involves the confidence and expectation that the thou in whom I believe, to whom I pledge and give myself totally, is worthy of my unconditional commitment.

The confidence included in belief, which he also refers to as an "assurance" *[II, 79]*, is not, he insists, a conviction even though it too is described as an "assurance" *[II, 76]*. The assurance in conviction is

8   HV, 143-44, 155-57. See also CF, 37; TW, 196-97.

9   My translation from French, ME, II, 80.

10   HV, 132-33; CF, 167.

centered on myself in that I maintain that nothing will change what I think no matter what the future brings. Faith's assurance, however, is centered on the thou in whom I believe and I cannot be certain that I will not cease to be faithful to that thou (and so "lose my faith"). Since my belief is a free act that "leaps" beyond any objective data I have, it is a risk or "a bet—and, like all bets, it can be lost" *[II, 79].*[11]

Marcel goes on to acknowledge that any particular belief, for example, in a banker to whom I entrust money, is always "open to the attack of primary reflection" *[II, 80],* which means that the justification of my confidence in him can be questioned and my belief may prove to be mistaken. However, "belief taken in its full or comprehensive reality," he maintains, is different and he offers as an illustration a mother who refuses to despair of her son but continues to believe, that is, to have confidence in and be committed to him in spite of all his deceptions and lies. The difference in the two cases, he states, is that the mother and her son have an "intersubjective bond" *[II, 81]* of love *[II, 82],* while the banker and I do not. Because of that bond, the mother is unable to view her son as an object separate from her which she can evaluate. In her love she commits herself unconditionally to be faithful to her child, to take care of him[12] and support him in becoming the person he should be. Furthermore, "taking care of" him is not something the mother simply wills to do without any reason (that is, "in a strictly voluntaristic sense"); rather, Marcel contends, her "voluntary act is staked on an affirmation of a different order ... [that is] properly speaking ontological" *[II, 82].*[13] Of course, to say that an affirmation is ontological is to say it is an affirmation of being, as a passage from *Concrete Approaches...* clearly affirms. There he writes, "if fidelity is possible it is because fidelity is ontological in its principle, because it draws on a presence that itself corresponds to a certain hold that being has upon us."[14] Similarly, in *Creative Fidelity* he states, "love is faith itself, an invincible assurance based on being itself" and, quoting from his early journals, he refers to

---

11   At TW, 33 and 146, Marcel insists that the assurance in faith does not mean certitude. At CF, 148, he calls faith a "vague assurance,."

12   I think that is a better translation of *pris en charge* (ME, II, 83) than "taking in charge."

13   My translation from French, ME, II, 83.

14   CA, 190.

"being as [the] ground of fidelity."[15] Thus, the mother wills to be faithful
to her wayward son, no matter how undeserving he shows himself to
be, because she affirms, or is assured of, the presence of being in him
which, as we have seen, is the dimension of him which she feels has
permanent, eternal value.

In what seems to be an aside, Marcel goes on to insist that the
mother's experience or assurance of being is not an intuition. For what
it's worth, I might point out that in other works he does describe faith
as an "immediate" consciousness of being[16] which means there are no
step by step mediatory processes one can go through to arrive at faith.
And he has no hesitation in calling that immediate consciousness an
intuition. He writes, "It seems to me that I am bound to admit that I
am—anyhow on one level of myself—face to face with Being," that is,
immediately aware of being, and he adds, "I think that an intuition of
this sort lies at the root of all fidelity."[17] Of course, whether or not he
uses the term intuition, his position seems clear. Faith is based on an
immediate experience of being, of that which is of permanent intrinsic
value. How else explain the mother's unyielding fidelity to her unworthy
child except that in her bond with him she experiences and feels assured,
at least implicitly or prereflectively, that he is a thou which has lasting
value?

Yet, her assurance, since it is not certitude, can be criticized as an
unjustified "pretension" and Marcel ends the chapter by responding to
that criticism [II, 82]. He describes pretension like conviction as "essentially centered on the I, the I who make the claim" that my conviction
about someone will not change [II, 83]. The pretension is that I have
categorized that individual accurately and he or she does not have the
freedom to move outside those categories. Of course, as we know, for
Marcel the assurance or confidence of faith is nonpretentious for it is
centered on, and open to, another being not on oneself. Such nonpre-
tentiousness seems almost a synonym for humility and so we can say

15   CF, 136, 170.

16   I believe he is referring to immediate consciousness on *MB, II, 82* when
he describes faith as "an assurance...an anticipation of something which,
discursively, could be reached only by successive steps" of mediation, for
faith is "a short cut across the zigzags of a mountain track."

17   BH, 98. The fact of the matter is that Marcel sometimes accepts and
sometimes rejects the term intuition to stand for an immediate nonreflective
awareness of being.

that "true love," and the fidelity that is part of it, are "humble" [II, 83].
In the next chapter, then, he will investigate humility.

Before leaving Chapter 5, however, I want to say more about Marcel's
concept of faith or fidelity and its ground in being for that topic is
something that he discusses in many works and some of them go into
more depth than he does here. Also, extending the discussion will enable
me to point out that in some of his reflections on fidelity he answers
questions he left unanswered in Volume I.

Let us first return to his distinction between a particular belief (for
example, in the honesty of a banker) and "belief taken in its full and
comprehensive reality" (illustrated by the mother) [II, 80]. No doubt our
confidence in the trustworthiness of a particular individual may prove
to be misplaced. Because our belief depended on that person behaving
in a certain way, for example, safeguarding our money, when he fails to
do so we cease to have confidence in or believe in him. When we come
to the mother, on the other hand, there is nothing her delinquent son
has done or can do to lose her love and fidelity. It is that kind of loving
fidelity, one which offers an unrestricted pledge of oneself to another,
that Marcel is most interested in. How is unconditional fidelity to a
creature possible, he wonders, and his answer is that unconditional faith
in a creature is possible only because one has faith in God, an absolute
Thou: "beginning with that absolute fidelity [to God] which we may
now simply call faith, the other fidelities [to creatures] become possible
... in faith and no doubt in it alone, these find their guarantee."[18]

We know that Marcel holds that being is the ground or basis of fidelity,
which means that fidelity is a response to "a reality, whether personal or
suprapersonal" which is experienced as having inherent value. But why
must fidelity to a finite reality or being involve faith in God? His argument, I believe, is the following. Only the presence of God, an absolute
Thou, can "guarantee" my unconditional faith in another creature for
only the presence of a personal or suprapersonal being who will always
be united to me in love can assure me that my total commitment to
another is not foolish. As he said earlier, I can offer an unconditional
pledge only because, implicitly at least, I feel I can always count on the
assistance I need to honor my pledge and only a loving God can assure
me of his unwavering assistance.[19] Furthermore, only to the extent that

---

18   CF, 167. See also, CF, 136-37.

19   HV, 133.

a creature participates in an eternal being of absolute value, and only a personal God who always loves me would be of absolute value, can I feel assured that this creature deserves an unconditional pledge of myself.[20]

Another way to show that God is necessary to account for fidelity to a creature, although I do not find it explicitly mentioned by Marcel, would be the following. Even though humans have permanent value, their value is nevertheless finite. Only the presence of a being of "infinite plenitude,"[21] a being possessing unlimited value, can call forth and deserve a *total* giving of my self. Thus, to repeat, only if I somehow experience a finite thou participating in a Being of infinite value, namely, an absolute Thou, does it make sense for me to offer that finite thou an unlimited and total commitment of loving fidelity.

Note by the way, that Marcel never tries to prove that people do unconditionally love and are faithful to others. He considers it a matter of experience that some human beings do pledge themselves absolutely to persons and causes. His intent, rather, is to understand how unconditional commitments to creatures are possible and his explanation, to repeat it once more, is that people commit themselves unconditionally to other finite beings only because they experience those beings participating in a being of unlimited value, a being who assures them that they will receive assistance to persevere in their commitments. Such a being would have to be a Thou of infinite love and value. Let me add quickly that Marcel does not believe that everyone who pledges unconditional fidelity and love must be a professed theist for the human awareness of God is always veiled and obscure and may remain entirely nonreflective or intuitive. A particular individual may simply not think about what is ultimately involved in his or her unlimited faithfulness to a spouse or child or close friend or cause. In fact, such an individual could even verbally profess atheism, Marcel says.[22] Nevertheless, only an assurance grounded in an encounter, however faint, with an absolute Thou can furnish the underpinnings of a person's unconditional commitment to

---

20 We shall see later that this confidence is rooted specifically in the belief that the creature is a gift from God.

21 Cf. 37.

22 He will discuss this later when he talks about naturally religious individuals.

another creature. "Unconditionality is a true sign of God's presence" he writes.[23]

Marcel's argument also explains some people's unwavering fidelity to causes. In last year's lectures, he wondered what must truth or justice or freedom be that some would be willing to sacrifice their lives for them? His initial response is that causes, such as justice or peace, cannot just be abstractions, for who would die or live for abstractions, but must be concretely embodied in persons or communities of persons.[24] Still, why commit oneself *unconditionally* to finite persons or communities of finite persons? Once again Marcel would say that it is because they are experienced, at least vaguely, to possess overwhelming value that causes embodied in persons call forth a total giving of one's self, and, in the final analysis, nothing could be of such value except an absolute Thou and what participates in that Thou.[25]

In Volume I Marcel also claimed that those who give their lives for a cause feel that their sacrifice is not absurd but meaningful for they believe that through their sacrifice they somehow achieve self-fulfillment not annihilation. We can now offer an explanation of their feeling. Such persons, he would claim, experience, perhaps only implicitly, their cause to participate in such a fullness of value that in giving themselves to it without reservation they unite with it and participate in that fullness *[II, 150]*. In other words, they and their causes participate in an absolute Thou, the being which fulfills their ontological exigency.

Yet there are other ways to interpret the experiences we have been discussing and Marcel admits it. He never claims that his phenomenological analyses offer a knock down, airtight, logically certain, demonstration of the presence of an absolute Thou in some human experiences. Because God's presence is veiled, it is always possible to interpret unconditional fidelity and love, and even the heroism of self-sacrifice, as self-deceptive and misguided and to maintain that the individuals in question did not actually experience, even prereflectively, being or an absolute Thou but only some finite, temporally limited, values in human creatures or causes, values that humans themselves create. Nor do they really experience

---

23 "Theism and Personal Relationships," in *Cross Currents*, I (1950-51), 40.

24 HV, 143-44, 155-57.

25 In Chapter 4 of Volume I, Marcel suspected that truth must be a person if someone could be faithful to it or betray it *(I, 89)*.

any power which would assist them in fulfilling their commitments. All that is just wishful thinking. Yet if that is true, the willingness of individuals who are well aware of their own inconstancy to dedicate themselves totally to values that are limited, temporary, human inventions, is perplexing, if not downright unintelligible. If the values in question will cease, if they are only human constructions which, therefore, can be deconstructed by human beings, why would anyone commit his or her self unconditionally to them? Those are the alternatives. Either those who pledge unlimited fidelity and love to creatures experience, at least dimly, divine assistance and something, or, better, someone, of unlimited value, or they are badly deluded and their commitments foolish and incomprehensible. One is free to choose either alternative, although the cynical one, Marcel points out, denigrates behavior that people of all ages have praised as embodying the highest virtues.[26]

Nevertheless, one might still balk at the above arguments by claiming that they prove too much. If, as Marcel argues, in order to account for our unconditional commitments to creatures we must affirm that we encounter in and through them a being who possesses overwhelming value and who will always assist us, then what about fanatics? People have been faithful to the point of death to all kinds of evil causes and persons, the Third Reich and Hitler, the classless society and Lenin, ethnic or religious supremacy and Osama bin Laden—and Marcel knows it.[27] In this country people died defending slavery. Now if some human beings have been willing to pledge unconditional fidelity and sacrifice everything for such people and causes, does his argument force him to the dubious conclusion that those people and causes also participate in overwhelming value and that individuals who totally dedicate themselves to them also experience the hidden presence of God in them? Surely, he would not grant that Hitler and his goals of racial purity participated in an absolute Thou, no matter how many sacrificed their lives for them. We will have to wait until Chapter 8, however, to see how he might respond to this most serious objection.

As I bring my commentary on Chapter 5 to a close, I also want to draw on works other than *The Mystery...* in order to briefly point out the connection Marcel makes between his concept of fidelity and the nature of the human self. Since to believe is to pledge *one's self* to another

---

26 CF, 146.

27 TW, 188, 196-97; MB, I, 89; MB, II, 167-68.

person or cause, it is not too much to say that I become my beliefs; belief is "in fact the foundation of what I am," he writes.[28] The commitments I make guide and shape my life and so I make my self in accord with what I believe in. For example, to the extent I believe in, that is, pledge myself to peace, I will live and act for peace and so form my self into a peacemaker. If I commit myself to pleasure in all its forms, I will make myself a hedonist. Yet we need to qualify this, for Marcel is also aware that the self I create through my commitments is not identically the self which believes. "Am I my belief as overtly manifested? Is my life identical with this belief?" he asks.[29] No, he replies, for I can judge that the self I have created inadequately measures up to my beliefs; although I do believe in peace, I am well aware that I do not fully live that commitment. Nevertheless, it remains true that I do, more or less successfully, create my self in accord with the persons or ideals I believe in and devote myself to. One more point. Since for Marcel to believe is to *unconditionally* pledge my self to be faithful, that is, to *always* be faithful to some person or cause, that demands that I recognize what he called in Volume I the deep dimension of my self which is supratemporal or eternal, that part of me which endures as me through all my changing temporal features.[30] Only if I recognize, at least implicitly, that I myself transcend time, can I pledge my self to be faithful to another beyond all temporal limits.

Finally, at the end of this lengthy commentary, it might be helpful if I briefly review how Marcel's treatment of faith or fidelity fits into this volume's investigations into being. In Chapter 4, he eventually came to focus his attention on the meaning of being when predicated of *a particular* being and especially on the being of another experienced in love. Because it experiences the being of the beloved, love proclaims to him or her, "thou at least, thou shalt not die" [II, 62], which means the lover *believes* in the immortality of the beloved. Since to rational thought that belief seems to be "a monstrous claim" [II, 70], Marcel decided in this chapter to investigate the nature of belief. He argued that unconditional fidelity or love pledged to a creature must be rooted in an experience of being, and ultimately in the, at least implicit, experience of a Being possessing unlimited value, namely an absolute Thou. At the conclusion

---

28 CF, 171.

29 CF, 172.

30 See my commentary on Chapter 9 of Volume I, 84-86 above.

of his investigation, he asserted that one of the characteristics of love and belief, which distinguish them from conviction and pretension, is that they are humble. That leads him to his next chapter devoted to humility and prayer.

Pages in other works of Marcel that treat material of this chapter:
CF, 120-37 and Chapter 8.
BH, 41-56, 95-99, 110-11, 199-212.
CA, 189-90.   HV, 125-34, 143-44, 155-57.
EBHD, 64-74, 99-100.   TW, 196-97.

6

PRAYER AND HUMILITY

Before I begin my commentary on this chapter, I want to point out that, from beginning to end, it deals with religious matters. By that I mean that Marcel reflects upon experiences, primarily humility and prayer, that are meaningful only insofar as they contain at least an implicit belief in some kind of a supreme being. Of course, since he adopts the phenomenological approach, it is perfectly legitimate for him to investigate the religious experiences of those who believe in God for such experiences are widespread. However, to call certain experiences religious does not mean that he thinks they are limited to professed theists or members of religious institutions. In Chapter 7 he will speak of the "naturally religious," persons who are not members of any organized religion and do not affirm any particular creed yet who do believe in and have some experience of the divine being. Thus, in addition to avowed believers Marcel believes that many people who have no professed faith or religion have religious experiences.

"True love is humble," Marcel stated at the end of Chapter 5 and now he undertakes an investigation into humility. He begins by distinguishing between self-humiliation and humility, explaining that the latter involves the recognition that "by myself I am nothing and I can do nothing except in so far as I am not only helped but promoted in my being by Him who is everything and all-powerful" [II, 85-86]. That means, as he defines it, humility "presupposes a certain affirmation of the sacred" [II, 86] and so, unlike modesty, is religious in character. Needless to say, humility is incompatible with technocracy or technomania which believe that technological methods apply to the whole range of human activities and that all questions, even about the meaning of life, the reality of God, and life after death, can be answered by the proper techniques—or, if they can't, then the questions are unanswerable.[1]

Marcel also distinguishes between humility and "that effacement of self which is implied by every objective knowledge" [II, 86-87]. The latter, so necessary for science, carefully guards against subjectively coloring the data or the results yielded by the empirical method. To

---

1   For more detail see Chapter 2 of Volume I.

insist on objectivity in science is to insist that one leave aside (abstract from) his or her personal likes and dislikes, values and disvalues; it is a methodological precaution against distorting the results of the empirical method. Humility is of "a different order; it is a mode of being," he asserts, which rejects any claim that "we are, or have the power to make ourselves dependent only upon ourselves" *[II, 87]*. Once again, he cautions against confusing humility and humiliation. Humility is "the act by which a human consciousness is led to acknowledge itself as tributary to something other than itself ... one from whom it holds its very being" *[II, 87-88]*[2] and the more one considers that something to be "an authentically transcendent reality," rather than a divinized state or some other human creation, the less will he or she be tempted to debase him or her self before it *[II, 89]*. By a "transcendent reality," Marcel explains elsewhere, he means a being which is absolutely beyond this world and, therefore, "something over which [we] can obtain no hold at all." He also calls that reality "the sacred or holy" which provokes in us feelings of "awe, love, and fear" and a reverent (or humble) posture of worship.[3] If we recognize that the sacred, the transcendent being to whom we owe everything, is an absolute Thou who is united in love with every human being, we can understand why he says that we should not debase ourselves before it for to do so would be to deny the inherent dignity of creatures that the transcendent Thou has created out of love and continues to hold dear.

One of the marks of authentic transcendence, Marcel goes on to say, is that it is connected to "true universality," both the "highest philosophical thought and the highest religious preaching" agree on this, he claims *[II, 90]*. The true or authentic universal does not mean something accepted by the masses for they can be swayed by powerful propaganda *[II, 99]*; rather, the universal he has in mind is a universality of values, such as truth, justice and loyalty. To label them universal is to claim that they are eternal values *[II, 99]*, that is, they are values that all human beings in every culture and historical period should adopt and live by. And the most fundamental universal value is the inherent worth and dignity of each and every human being without exception.[4]

---

2   My translation from French, ME, II, 88.

3   BH, 187. My translation from the French, *Être et Avior*, 277.

4   HV, 26-29, 155-60; EBHD, 148; MAMS, 53-54, 66, 70, 268.

Marcel knows that some contemporary thinkers maintain that values are purely subjective, that they are simply what certain human beings choose and prefer. But, he counters, if that were true the result would be a moral relativism which would "eventually tend to annul, to annihilate, the affirmations of moral conscience" *[II, 93]* for no values like truth and justice would universally apply to all human beings, and that, "would be the end of man and of the order which in the course of history he has tried ... to establish" *[II, 92]*. If nothing, including human persons, possesses *inherent* value, if all values are simply human preferences, then people can prefer slavery, genocide, rape and war and they will have value! To insist, on the contrary, that all human persons are *intrinsically* valuable, is to say with Kant that persons "should be treated as ends in themselves," their worth is not simply the product of human choices. Marcel affirms his agreement with Kant's famous principle and suggests that it arose in "a mental climate soaked in the Christian spirit" *[II, 93]*, a climate that embedded the belief that every human person possesses inherent worth and dignity because he or she has been created and redeemed by a loving God. I think that belief is what he is referring to when he states that "a connection" must be maintained "between authentic transcendence and true universality" *[II, 91]*. He expresses it very clearly in his *Metaphysical Journal* where he writes that "the real spirit of universality," namely, the inherent dignity of all human beings, "which is the religious spirit in eminent degree, is only realized by belief in the divine fatherhood."[5] Kant himself did not recognize the concrete influence of Christianity on his view that persons are ends in themselves, Marcel claims, but, in any case, the perspective of our contemporaries is no longer within "a mental climate soaked in the Christian spirit" *[II, 93]*—and he does not think that change of perspective constitutes progress.

These considerations, he continues, may enable us to obtain a better view of the nature of the pure venerable or reverential (elsewhere called the sacred), which is essential for understanding true humility *[II, 94]*. The venerable which is present in authentic religion "implies distance," he states, which no doubt refers to what he earlier called "an authentic transcendent reality," a reality, he says here, that one can worship *[II, 95]*. Accordingly, he criticizes contemporary sociologists who deny the transcendent side of religion by reducing it to subjective phenomena such as the adoration present in those who belong to certain religious

5   MJ, 88. In MAMS he makes exactly the same statement, 258-59.

groups. For one thing, he points out, faith in God is a *personal* choice and, as Kierkegaard recognized, a choice which may be in opposition to the beliefs held by members of religious groups. For another, the true religious community with which I unite myself even if I pray alone, "does not belong exclusively, or even primarily, to the visible world" and so is beyond the range of "objective sociology" *[II, 95]* which studies observable religious institutions.

Having just mentioned prayer, Marcel turns his attention to it for, he declares, "it is the essential datum" of religion *[II, 96]*. (Needless to say, true prayer includes what he has just discussed, humility and reverence before a transcendent being.) Although we have no right, he says, to stipulate what forms prayer must take, we can investigate the meaning of the terms pure and impure when attributed to prayers. We tend to believe a prayer is more pure the less selfish it is, the more it is for someone else, and, to be sure, for me not to appeal to God's mysterious power on behalf of another would mean I lack love and fidelity for that other. Yet if I am personally attached to the being I love, "my prayer [for him or her] could always be looked upon as somewhat selfish" *[II, 97]*. Not so, Marcel responds, to claim that my love for another is more authentic or pure "according as I love less for my own sake ... and more for the sake of the other" implies "too dualist a notion of the lover and loved," for love consists of a "more and more indivisible community, in the bosom of which I and the other tend to be continually more perfectly absorbed" *[II, 98]*. As we saw in Volume I, love for Marcel is a *union* of lover and loved, a participation of each in the reality of the other;[6] therefore, for the lover to pray for his beloved's well being is at one and the same time for him to pray for his own well-being—for they have become one.

Next he addresses the objection that it may be arbitrary to claim that "the selfish request is spiritually speaking inferior to that which is made on behalf of another" since "we do not yet know what are true values" and must wait for scientific progress to enlighten us *[II, 98]*. To this, he retorts that science, no matter how well developed, "can tell us nothing about values" *[II, 99]*. Its objective approach can reveal only certain factual conditions and, at best, what certain societies or individuals judge to be good or bad; science cannot not say what values people *should* or *should not* profess. Even stronger, if one day science asserted the primacy of selfishness over unselfishness that would be a "most

---

6   *I, 177-81.*

terrifying retrogression" in our moral conscience, Marcel contends *[II, 100]*. I presume he says that because in a society comprised of moral egoists, each individual would judge the good to be only that which benefits him or her and serious conflicts would arise when people's judgments fundamentally disagreed. A war of all against all could well result which would end only when some became powerful enough to impose their values forcibly on others.

Now if the impure or less pure prayer is one that is self-centered, can we then say, Marcel asks, "that the God to whom that prayer is addressed does not exist"—while the God of pure or authentic prayer does exist? Before directly addressing those questions, he reflects "on the use of the words *existence* and *nonexistence* when they are meant to apply to a being who cannot form part of the web of our experience" *[II, 108]*. It seems clear from both his use of the term existence and the discussion which follows that by "experience" he means sensory experiences of "the empirical world" *[II, 100]*[7] and, of course, God is not an empirical object that can be "part of the web of our experience"of that world. However, Marcel appears to go even further by asserting that we must not even "ask ourselves whether *there is* or is not someone in whom we could find certain attributes which would allow us to qualify him as God." Yet he also states, it would also be unreasonable to claim "as the atheists claim that *there is no one* who has such attributes" *[II, 101]*. On their face, his statements are perplexing since he himself has certainly assigned attributes to God by speaking of him as an absolute Thou, as transcendent, and as sacred. Nevertheless, he proceeds to advance still another paradox by stating that it is absurd to consider "the person who prays as addressing himself to someone who receives his prayer" yet it is equally wrong "to maintain that the individual who prays does so 'in the void'" *[II, 101]*. Fortunately, he clarifies his meaning by explaining that the oppositions he has enunciated have "value and even meaning only in the *empirical* order" *[II, 101]*,[8] which means they refer to a God conceived as an empirical object.

In trying to reconcile the above contradiction which rejects both the idea that prayer is addressed to someone who receives it and the idea that one prays in the void, we might be tempted to think that the act of

---

7   My translation from French, ME, II, 100.

8   My emphasis and translation from French, ME, II, 101.

praying "contains in itself its own response, its own fulfillment" *[II, 101].*[9] But that can't be true, he argues, because those who pray most fervently testify that the exigency which prompts their prayers seeks a response from a being beyond themselves and so depends "on the mysterious will of an incomprehensible power whose plans we cannot fathom" *[II, 102].* However, if prayer is uncertain about the response it will receive from such a power, perhaps it is deluded in believing there is such a power in the first place—and "it is the philosopher's business to expose and denounce this delusion." Marcel rejects that alternative since it would give "primacy to philosophy in matters that concern religious life" and that would end up depreciating religion by reducing it to something human reason can comprehend and verify. "The philosophy of existence," he states, "cannot but be completely dissatisfied with such a devaluation" *[II, 102].* Since that kind of philosophy proceeds by reflecting upon lived experience, in this case the religious experience of the believer, it must, therefore, allow believers' experiences to have the last word. And when his prayer is pure, the believer cannot think of it as being unanswered and that is because, "the believer cannot not[10] feel assured that he has a living relation with God," even though he does not know "the manner in which empirically his prayer will be granted" *[II, 102].* To have a living relation with God, Marcel explains, means that authentic prayer is a "very humble and fervent way of *uniting oneself with* ... something which infinitely transcends me" *[II, 103].* In other words, the praying believer participates in the mysterious transcendent power to whom he or she humbly prays and that union is the basis of the believer's assurance that his or her prayer will be heard and answered by that incomprehensible transcendent power, which is, of course, an absolute Thou.

That raises another question: how is it possible for a finite human being to unite with a being that infinitely transcends it? Marcel rejects the idea that the union be interpreted as a surrender to the unknown *will* of God for, while it is true that the believer does humbly assume a posture of "absolute submission [to] a being in whom he has faith," that should not be interpreted as submission to God's *will* because it is "extremely difficult for us to distinguish what is willed and is only permitted" by God *[II, 103].* Yet that distinction is crucial lest we absurdly

---

9   My translation from French, ME, II, 102.

10   Correcting the English translation of French, ME, II, 102. The translation leaves out the second "not"!

think that everything, every disease and every human action, even the most heinous, is willed by God. In this matter, he states, we must "force our way between two errors" *[II, 104]*.

One error would be to think that everything that happens, including prayer, is necessarily determined by the divine will or some other causal chain. If that were true, Marcel argues, prayer would simply be "a pure epiphenomenon or rather autosuggestion" *[II, 104]* because it would have no independent reality or efficacy of its own but would be nothing but a necessary effect of certain causes. The other error would be to pretend that there are no necessary causal connections at all in nature. The truth is that we must try to see how the "spirit of prayer" can fit together with the necessary operations of natural causes ("series of positive steps") disclosed by human reason in a given situation *[II, 104]*. Marcel offers the example of a person with an incurable disease. Rather than viewing it just as the inevitable effect of an objective chain of causes over which he has no control, and so becoming stoically indifferent about it, that person could view the disease as a "situation which presents to him something of fundamental importance" *[II, 105]*.[11]

In last year's lectures Marcel mentioned that illness could be something that is viewed as part of my situation, that is, something joined to my very being which affects me both internally and externally. Yet, he also said that I am free to choose my "attitude" toward that situation. Similarly an incurable disease, even if its contraction and progress are beyond my control, is also part of my "situation," meaning that it is something in which I participate and it affects my very being, and I remain free to decide how I will react to it. Those with the spirit of prayer may choose to consider their disease as a test from God, as purification of their soul, as punishment for sin, or as a means of joining with the sufferings of others. Whatever their choice, they will not view their illness with stoic indifference, as an object separate from themselves, but will regard it as part of their being as well as something whose meaning depends on the attitude they choose to adopt.

As for defining "the spirit of prayer," Marcel describes it both negatively and positively. Negatively, it is a rejection of the temptation to self-centeredness; positively, it is "a receptive disposition towards everything which can detach me from myself" and open me to others *[II, 105]*. Accordingly, he denies that the spirit is an "interior disposition" which is entirely within me, for "prayer is possible only when intersubjectivity is

---

11   My translation from French, ME, II, 105.

recognized, where it is in actuality" *[II, 106].*[12] He repeats what he stated above, prayer is not an "*external* relation between the person who prays and the person who hears his prayer;" it is rooted in an intersubjective union of a person with God. Clearly, then, the spirit of prayer includes a receptive disposition toward a union with a holy, transcendent being. Now since intersubjectivity is not a structure that can be empirically verified, Marcel grants that we are always free to deny its reality and claim, as in solipsism, that we have no access to the reality of another, whether that other be human subjects or God. But, he adds, he is almost certain "there is nobody who has all his life been so unlucky" as to never have experienced an intersubjective relation with another *[II, 107]*. Presumably, anyone who has had that kind of relationship with a human thou could be open to the possibility of an encounter with an absolute Thou.

We now have all the elements of his answer to the question he posed: how is it possible for a finite being to unite with a being that infinitely transcends it? Marcel's response is that we must conceive such a union as intersubjective, that is, as a spiritual union of a finite I and absolute Thou. To say that God infinitely transcends the finite creature is not to say that a loving union between them is impossible, especially if it is initiated by absolute Love. In *Creative Fidelity* he writes that God is "more internal to me than myself" and says that it is "in terms of love that this can be understood"[13] and he refers to my "participation in a reality which overflows and envelops me" without being in any way external to me.[14] The point is that when he speaks of the transcendent Marcel does not claim it is utterly beyond all human engagement or experience; on the contrary, the transcendent God *is* experienced in humble adoration and authentic prayer as something sacred, awesome, completely beyond human control, and as a reality on whom we are totally dependent.

Finally, note that in this chapter Marcel has described experiences of God that are somewhat different from those he presented in previous chapters. Earlier he argued that the only way to explain how and why we offer unconditional pledges of love and fidelity to other creatures is to admit that we encounter in and through them an absolute Thou. Here his focus is on God experienced in humility and prayer as a sacred, transcendent, all powerful being which we cannot command, from whom

---

12   My translation from French, ME, II, 106.

13   CF, 100. See also BH, 125.

14   CF, 144.

we receive all we are. And let me repeat what I said in the beginning of my commentary on this lecture. When Marcel claims that humble and prayerful persons experience and participate in a holy, transcendent being on which they are completely dependent, he does not mean that all such people are *explicitly* aware of encountering such a being nor of their own lived humility and prayer. Of course, even those who are in some way aware of experiencing a transcendent being may not belong to the same, or to any, religion or have the same, or any, description of the transcendent. In *Tragic Wisdom...* he writes, "something sacred, whose nature remains to be determined, can exist for individuals who refuse all ritualism and belong to no church"[15] and in *Searchings* he goes even further by stating that "even nonbelievers, or, more precisely people who do not regard themselves believers, can also experience it ["the sacral" or "the holiness of God"]."[16] The latter may experience the sacred transcendent being only vaguely and prereflectively and, therefore, may not be expressly aware that they do so. Nevertheless, persons whose lives manifest a humble recognition of their absolute dependence upon a power wholly beyond the human, a power they invoke in unformulated prayers, must at least faintly experience the transcendent.[17] Otherwise their lived humility and unvoiced supplications make no sense. As always, we are free to accept the religious person's experience of the transcendent or to reject it, since it is far from overwhelmingly clear or unambiguous; after all, we are talking about faith not certitude. Nevertheless, some kinds of experiences of the transcendent, no matter how obscure and elusive, have been claimed by peoples of all cultures and periods of history. To dismiss or denigrate them is to reject experiences that many, if not most, human beings believe touch the ultimate depth of reality.

Pages in other works of Marcel that treat material of this chapter:
CF, 48-50, 167.   HV, 26-28, 132, 155-60.
BH, 187-89.   TW, 109-19, 211.   MJ, 86-89, 223-26, 264-68.

---

15   TW, 109.

16   *Searchings*, 42.

17   As one illustration, Marcel mentions his contemporary, the German philosopher, Martin Heidegger, whom he met a number of times and who, even though he claimed that he was neither a theist nor an atheist, did experience, Marcel believes, "that being is a sacral reality," TW, 243. See also *Awakenings*, 193.

7
FREEDOM AND GRACE

Marcel begins by repeating that prayer involves intersubjectivity and adds that for the Christian that relationship is provided by the Church, viewed not objectively as an institution but as "*agape* or as incarnate intersubjectivity." What is more, just as a person may be a theist and reflectively be unaware of it, so a person can belong to the Church and not be explicitly conscious of it. Individuals can unknowingly be in the Church if they sympathetically detect in it "a mode of intersubjective presence from which the Church derives her value and significance" *[II, 108]*. The key word here is "sympathetically" for it indicates that the individuals have some degree of union or participation in the incarnate intersubjective presence which comprises the Church. Of course, I am free to deny that intersubjective presence or to recognize it, Marcel grants, and that brings him to the major topic of this chapter—-freedom, which he states has been presupposed from the beginning of the second series of lectures. (As we shall see, the term freedom has a number of different but related meanings for him.)

From a religious perspective it might be objected that a choice to recognize the intersubjective character of the Church depends more on grace, a divine gift, than on human freedom and that suggests, Marcel remarks, that the real problem here is the "intimate relation which must be established between gift and freedom, between freedom and grace." Indeed, the way we conceive of that difficult relation is very important because it will determine whether we can "take a position about the existence of God"[1] or philosophically articulate some solution to the question of being *[II, 109]*.

Proceeding phenomenologically, Marcel reflects on our "own living experience" and asks, "to what extent ... can I or can I not assert that I am a free being?" *[II, 109]*.[2] But what exactly do I mean by that question and in particular by the term freedom? I might interpret freedom as "doing what I want to do," but, he points out, there are many instances where I do not do what I want to do and still am free. We can understand why

---

1   My translation from French, ME, II, 110.

2   I have slightly modified the translation from French, ME, II, 110.

he says that if we substitute the word desire for want—then freedom means "whether or not I do what I desire." But that is not freedom for I experience myself to be free only when I use "my will in opposition to my own desire," rather than give in to its temptations and seductions [II, 110]. Furthermore, some people in captivity, who can not possibly do what they want or desire, have a deep experience of their inner freedom, he claims. The issue is even more complicated for suppose I realize that in some circumstance I have yielded to my desires although I should not have. Could I excuse myself by claiming that I did not act freely because "a power independent of my will tyrannized me and I was forced to obey?" Marcel replies that there is something in me which protests against my placing in something else "the responsibility for what was in spite of everything my own act" [II, 111] and I have a feeling that if I excused myself by attributing such power to my desires, I would place myself more and more at their mercy.

What, then, is that inner me and what is its freedom, he asks? Of course, neither is an object which we can observe from the outside like things. If we think of ourselves on the model of things "we make it impossible for ourselves, by definition, to attach the least meaning to the word freedom" [II, 112], because the world of things is ruled by determinism, meaning that every natural event has a cause which necessitates it and that cause a cause which necessitates it, and so forth. Yet, freedom should not be thought in opposition to causal determinism either, Marcel states, "it lies in a completely different plane." Rather than trying to consider my freedom as some thing I can observe from outside, it "must be something I decide. ... [I] assert my freedom, and this assertion is bound up with the consciousness that I have of myself" [II, 113]. To explain what he means, he quotes a passage from a contemporary German philosopher, who states that our consciousness of our freedom comes when we realize that it is up to us whether we will fulfill or avoid our obligations to others. In other words, we become aware that we ourselves have to make the decision about those obligations, "and so about ourselves," and that we are responsible for the decision we make and for what we become through that decision [II, 113].

Moving to a different point, Marcel contends that freedom can not "be thought of as a predicate which somehow belongs to man considered in his essence," even though we do express ourselves that way when we assert "I am free." He admits that there is a sense in which "to say, 'I am free' is to say, 'I am I'" [II, 114] but, still, that should be said cautiously for "if we examine ourselves carefully, we must admit that there are countless circumstances" in which we are not free but behaving automatically, or following the crowd, or acting out an obsession, or, as said above, acting as the slave of our desires. The fact of the matter is, he says elsewhere, "freedom is a conquest," that is, "every one of us has to make himself into a free man" for we are not "*born free*"[3] or "essentially" free.

These remarks, Marcel says, should prepare us to understand that freedom is not "essentially freedom of choice" when that is "conceived as indeterminism" [II, 115]. Since he believes choice would be the most free "when the reasons for choosing one way or the other are the least strong," he interprets freedom of choice or indeterminism to imply that freedom pertains only to insignificant matters[4] when, on the contrary, "the free act is essentially a significant act" because it is an act that "helps to make me what I am;" it involves the "creation of myself by myself" [II, 116-17], rather than the creation of myself by forces I have no control over.

Marcel turns next to the relation between freedom and grace. Before going there, however, I will try and put together his different notions of freedom, some of which he has rather summarily presented here, and I will supplement what he says in *The Mystery...* with his treatment of freedom in other works. Though it sounds paradoxical, Marcel holds that freedom is both something we in some sense are and something we must become. To make sense of that I suggest that we distinguish in his thought between the self as *fundamental* freedom and the self as freedom *to be achieved*; the terminology is mine. He has the latter in mind when he encourages us to become individuals who free ourselves from self-centeredness, become disposable to others, and enter into intersubjective relations with them.[5] In addition, as he suggested above [II, 110], we become free by gaining sovereignty over ourselves by achieving control of our desires and passions so that "the willed has preeminence over the suffered."[6] Those who become free in this sense are not at the mercy of factors outside or within themselves; they themselves through their

---

3   EBHD, 146. See also 152.

4   To my knowledge, few philosophers equate indeterminism and indifference. For most, to say a free choice is indeterminate simply means that it is not determined, not necessitated.

5   CF, 51-53; MAMS, 24; EBHD, 147.

6   EBHD, 154; MAMS, 17-18,

own wills are in control. The other kind of freedom, our fundamental freedom, is *"our freedom that is ourselves"* for it *is* part of our being,[7] Marcel states, and it "grasps itself first as a simple power of affirmation and denial."[8] Our fundamental freedom is the "creative power"[9] by which I decide what kind of a person I will become, one in control of, or enslaved to, my desires, one open to others or self-centered, and so forth. That freedom is a creative power which "incarnates itself or... becomes a real power of conferring a content on itself;"[10] in other words, it is a power by which I create myself. Consciousness of that basic freedom comes, as he noted above, when I realize that to some extent[11] it is up to me, it is my responsibility, to decide what I will become. Now may I point out that my fundamental freedom which is a "power of affirmation and denial" is in fact the power to freely choose among alternatives and it is not the freedom of indifference that Marcel rejected earlier. In fact, as he said in the beginning of this chapter, he has presupposed the existence of that kind of freedom throughout these lectures. He has, for example, insisted that we have the freedom to chose to accept our obligations to others or not, to interpret unconditional fidelity and love as nonsense or as rooted in an encounter with being, to follow our vocation or reject it, to believe in God or not, to engage in secondary reflection or stay on the level of primary—-to name just a few instances. We are even free, he says, to accept our fundamental freedom or to pretend we are determined *[II, 111-12]*.[12] This basic freedom which is our selves is, I believe, part of that supratemporal or eternal dimension of our selves discussed last year in Chapter 9, *[I, 190-95]*. In that dimension of ourselves our "ruling principle" (called the will above) attempts to control the

---

7   CF, 55.

8   CF, 26, my translation from the French, *Essai de philosophie concrète*, 44.

9   CF, 96.

10   CF, 26.

11   I say "to some extent" since it is obvious that not everything I become is the result of my freedom. My innate capacities and talents are given and my personal development can be severely restricted or enhanced by the situations of my life, many of which I have little control over. Recall Marcel's discussions of the impact of my situation and of others on me, *(I, Chapter 7* and *9, II, Chapter 1)*.

12   CF, 100-01.

details of our "life processes;" it is also that part of us which, because it is permanent, we can freely choose to commit to others in unconditional love and fidelity.[13] Finally, our fundamental freedom is in some sense the most central feature of our eternal selves for Marcel since it is the creative power which is the enduring source of whatever we become. As if to emphasize its primacy, he describes it as "that freedom which is somehow the soul of our soul."[14]

Let us turn now to his discussion of the relation between freedom and grace or gift. "What is a gift?" Marcel asks, and he answers that it is not a transfer of something which must be returned, rather it has "a certain character of unconditionalness" [II, 118]. Since it is unconditional, a gift is generous: "The soul of a gift is its generosity" [II, 118], he declares, and he describes it using his favorite metaphor of light. Generosity is like "a light whose joy is in giving light, in being light" [II, 119], that is, like an illuminating light which wishes to be more so, generosity seeks to increase. One advantage of using the term light, Marcel claims, is that it allows us to interpret "experiences as different as those of the artist, the hero, or the saint" for those experiences can all be interpreted as experiences of radiance, a radiance that emanates from being itself "grasped in his [the hero's] act, his [the saint's] example or his [the artist's] work" [II, 120].[15] In other words, we can experience the radiance of the light which is being in the work of the artist, the act of the hero, and the example of the saint. Since light enables us to see values [II, 124], and since, as we know, being is that which possesses intrinsic value, the radiance of light that emanates from being and that we grasp in the three illustrations must be the respective values they manifest to us. Marcel's words about radiance may also mean that the artist himself experiences value or the radiance of being in the work to be produced, the hero in the act to be done, and the saint in the life of virtue which is an example to others, and, insofar as they remain true to those respective values, they radiate or manifest the light of being to others.

Continuing to discuss the relation of generosity and gift, Marcel states that "it is generosity which makes the 'gift' possible" [II, 120] and that, in fact, generosity itself seems to be a gift. To say that it is a gift,

---

13 BH, 42.

14 CF, 55.

15 My translation from French, ME, II, 121.

he explains, means it is not a result which can be attained through the efforts of oneself or others: "A gift ... is not a result, it arises spontaneously." Furthermore, just as light is recognized only because it illuminates something which radiates it, "so generosity can be discerned only through the gifts it lavishes." Yet if I am to be certain that a gift has been lavished on me, such as an inborn talent or my life itself, I need, he claims, a "formal assurance," such as a word, whether written or not, from the giver *[II, 121]*. Now what word could that be, he asks, and replies that there is only one possibility, "this word can only be a revelation"[16] and "it is only in so far as I somehow become gratefully conscious of this revelation that I can come to apprehend life and my own life as a gift." And he immediately adds, "this apprehension can exist without my being articulately and distinctly conscious of the Revelation as such" and "this is the case of those whom one may call naturally religious beings" *[II, 122]*. We described the "naturally" religious in an earlier chapter but not its connection with revelation. Note that in Marcel's first mention of revelation above the term has a small "r," while the later citation uses a capitol "R." "Revelation" refers to specific religions (such as Christianity, Judaism, Hinduism, and Islam) and particular beliefs about God's revelation derived from their sacred books, creeds, ceremonies, and traditions. The former, revelation with a small r, while it too is from God, involves no particular religion or beliefs, no sacred books, creeds, or traditions and so it can be given to those "unfamiliar with any form of positive religion."[17] It can be present in those who are not reflectively and explicitly aware of God's reality or of being enlightened by what Marcel calls the metaphysical light "of which St. John speaks as enlightening every man who comes into the world" *[II, 121]*. Such individuals, of course, are the "naturally religious" and, insofar as their beliefs in God may be entirely on the prereflective level of experience, they could even be "professed" atheists! In a number of works, Marcel distinguishes between professed and lived atheists.[18] *Verbal* atheism, professed by those whose lives bear witness to their belief that life is a gift, that it is not just a chance event in a purposeless universe but is ultimately good and meaningful, is not incompatible with a veiled,

---

16 The term revelation used here is not capitalized in French, (ME, II, 123), and that is very significant.

17 CA, 196.

18 TW, 42-44, 166-69; CF, 77-80, 182; *Searchings*, 42.

obscure, nonreflective experience of God—which could be called *lived* theism. Surely we can observe that many human beings, not just avowed theists, have experiences, such as those "which give rise to the *gaudium essendi*, the joy of existing."[19] Such experiences may occur on the birth of one's child, the discovery that one's love for another is returned, or any encounter with "the richness of the universe,"[20] Marcel notes. At such times it is natural for us to rejoice in our existence and for feelings of gratitude to arise spontaneously in our hearts, whether or not we are overt theists, gratitude in response to the gift of life, a gift, whether we realize it or not, that can come only from a loving Creator.

To put it succinctly, Marcel maintains that only God's revelation can account for the fact that some human beings experience life to be a gift, that is, to be something intrinsically meaningful and valuable that has been bestowed on us. And that revelation has been given to all those who show by their actions that they recognize that life possesses inherent worth. His reasoning is perfectly straightforward. Who other than a God conceived as the source of all that is could reveal to us, whether in words or not, that our existence is not a freak accident of blind cosmic evolution but something of enormous significance? Note that his argument is very similar to the one he gave earlier in Chapter 4 which maintained that only if we experience an absolute Thou can we make sense of our feeling that something of imperishable value, something or someone deserving our total, unconditional love and fidelity, is present in our fellow human beings and in the causes to which we commit ourselves. In both cases I believe Marcel would claim that our experiences of such astounding values in ourselves or others is our experience of God's revelation, where the term revelation is used to emphasize that only divine generosity, not our human efforts or merit, can ultimately account for the presence of such values in creatures.

Now, since the experience of God's revelation that life is a gift is not overpowering nor accompanied with absolute certitude, Marcel grants that we are free to deny it and interpret our lives as "absurd phenomena," freak happenings in the meaningless history of matter *[II, 122]*. Does that mean that we are left with an "arbitrary choice between two conceptions of which it cannot rationally be claimed that one is more true than another?" *[II, 123]*. It is very difficult, if not impossible, he

---

19   TW, 42. See also, HV, 43.

20   TW, 43; CF, 143.

concedes, to *demonstrate* that the negative interpretation, that life is absurd, is false. On the other hand, he argues, is it not a "self-destructive" position for if our lives have no ultimate sense, how can truth, even the alleged truth that our lives lack meaning, retain any significance? No doubt, some may freely choose to be satisfied with, and perversely enjoy, that self-destruction and there is no way to refute them if they lack good will—by which I presume he means, at least, the willingness to be open to the revelation of evidence contrary to their position *[II, 124]*.

Furthermore, if good will is lacking, what value could freedom itself have, he asks, and he goes on to stress the essential connection between freedom and truth, implying that the value of freedom comes in its acknowledging the value of truth. To see freedom and truth as values, he adds, one has to "place himself ... within the intelligible light" which "is at the root of all and every understanding" *[II, 124]*, apparently referring again to the "Light which enlightens every man" by illuminating or revealing the inherent value and meaning in truth, freedom and life itself. The lecture ends here without explicitly tying together freedom and gift or grace, although he does imply that, just as our lives are gifts, so also is our freedom. In *Creative Fidelity* he asserts that clearly.[21] My "freedom is a gift," he writes, from an absolute Thou who "invites me to create myself." Yet that gift is so unconditionally granted to me that I can "accept *or refuse it*," and one way of refusing it, he says, is to refuse to acknowledge its source and to "persist in maintaining that I belong only to myself."

As I bring my commentary on this chapter to a close, I want to return to two items Marcel mentioned earlier in these lectures, one in this chapter and one in Chapter 2. Early in this lecture he stated that understanding the relation between freedom and gift was crucial for taking a position about the existence of God *[II, 109]*. We have now seen him argue that only God's revelation, whether written or not, can explain why we experience life to be a gift and that, therefore, to experience life as ultimately valuable and meaningful is to experience, however vaguely and dimly, God as its source. We have also seen him admit that the experience in question is uncertain and unclear for a gift is not something we are forced to accept, which means we are free to acknowledge God's revelation and hence his reality, or to ignore or reject it. Our freedom, then, has the last word when it comes to taking

21 CF, 100-01. See also, 54-55.

a position on God's existence. I should add that we shall see later that the role of our freedom in deciding whether or not God exists is even more significant than might first appear since Marcel doubts that any intellectual demonstrations or proofs of God's existence are possible.

The second point refers to his notion of vocation which he first discussed last year. At that time he left open the question of the source of our vocation or ideal self, the self we feel called and even obliged to become. Earlier in this series, in Chapter 2, he asserted (without explanation) that my being—in the context that meant my ideal self or vocation—was a *gift* [II, 32]. Now in this present chapter we have seen him argue that to designate something as a gift means that it is not something humans themselves can create or merit and that is why only God's revelation can account for our experience that life is a gift, that is, possesses intrinsic meaning and value. I submit that the same thing could be said about our vocation for as an ideal, it is a self which possesses value, a self that we did not do anything to deserve nor did we produce—-for, insofar as we experience it as obligatory, even against our wishes, we experience it to be not our own creation. (As I have said, if we created it ourselves we could just construct a different vocation if the first became too demanding, but that is precisely what we feel we must not do if we are to be true to our calling to become better selves.) Since our vocation, our ideal self, possesses value that we did not confer on it, a value that may even call us to sacrifice our lives, its source must be God, the Light which offers that gift of light by which I can, and should, evaluate and guide my life.

Pages in other works of Marcel that treat material of this chapter:
TW, 42-43, 84-87, 241-42.
CF, 26, 30-31, 51-55, 77-80, 100-01, 143-44.
EBHD, 144-60.   MAMS, Chapter 1.   HV, 19.

8

TESTIMONY

Chapter 8 begins with Marcel stating that the analyses of the preceding chapter should help us avoid thinking of grace as a mode of causality distinct from the causality of a human agent. Here and elsewhere he seems to consider causality to be a determined relation between empirical objects; a cause is an empirical thing that necessarily produces another empirical thing.[1] Obviously, grace is not a cause in that sense for it is not an empirical thing and when it is given to human beings it leaves them free to accept it or not. He then returns to a question posed toward the end of the previous chapter: "is there any meaning in maintaining that I am wrong when my *being in the world* appears to me as the expression of a generosity of which it is the embodiment?" *[II, 125]*. Of course, the atheist claims that there is no one who bestows that alleged gift, but Marcel responds that what the atheist means is that it is impossible to *verify* that an identifiable empirical cause of my being exists. The believer who maintains life is a gift, however, is not referring to a cause that can be identified and verified within the empirical world but to a nonempirical, "nonidentifiable as such," and that "non-identifiable is experienced or apprehended as the absolute Thou" *[II, 126]*.[2]

Of course, that prompts another question, is there any reality beyond the empirically verifiable and falsifiable? To answer, Marcel does not attempt to logically demonstrate the existence of a nonempirical supreme being; rather, he reflects on his own concrete faith experience of an absolute Thou. In doing so, he admits that there are times when "there

---

1   *Problematic Man*, trans, Brian Thompson (New York: Herder and Herder, 1967), 54-55, 58, 60; MJ, 35.

2   By verification Marcel means "empirical verification" (CF, 61). I might point out that when these lectures were given a very dominant Anglo-American philosophical movement was Logical Positivism. That position held that only statements which were empirically verifiable were meaningful, that is, only propositions which directly or indirectly entailed something that could be observed by the senses, unaided or aided by instruments. That meant, of course, that any statements about nonempirical entities were literally meaningless.

as he just said, the openness to being penetrated by being (light) and the ability to disseminate its radiance.

As for that last point, Marcel understands that I might wonder if I actually have a power of dissemination but he responds that I can be certain that I am able to show forth being (or disseminate light) because to some degree "I am a living testimony" or witness to being or light already *[II, 129]*. He recognizes that he needs to explain that statement and so decides "to delve further into the essence of testimony" or of bearing witness.

On the empirical level, testimony is possible only if I have been the witness of some historical occurrence for, then, I can give my word or oath that I was present when it happened—and since the event is now past my testimony may be indispensable *[II, 130]*. But, can we not testify or bear witness to ideals, such as justice or truth, that are beyond time? Marcel thinks not. To bear witness to justice or peace or any other ideal, he claims, seems "possible only insofar as the idea has been embodied" in an historical situation *[II, 131]*, as when we work here and now to free the innocent or to combat error. Apparently his position here is the same as his stance on fidelity to causes. No one would ever sacrifice his or her self for an abstraction, he said earlier; peace or justice must be embodied in human persons or communities of persons to be worthy of our fidelity.

Consistent with his insistence on the historical character of testimony, Marcel states that faith "can be testimony only of the living God" *[II, 131]*, that is, a God who is not a timeless, unchanging being but can in some way be present in history and encountered there. Even more, a living God must also in some way be concretely related to every human being "who is my neighbor" so that every "approach to justice...or to charity in the person of my neighbor, is at the same time an approach to this God himself" *[II, 130]*. Otherwise, he claims, God would be only an atemporal unchanging idea "against whom I cannot sin" *[II, 132]* by choosing to betray or be unfaithful to my neighbor.[7]

Needless to say, the God incarnated in history proclaimed by Christianity immediately comes to mind as does the testimony to that God offered by faithful witnesses throughout the centuries. The reference to Christianity gives Marcel the opportunity to distinguish, once again,

---

7   I do not understand why Marcel limits testimony or faith to temporal matters. It seems to me one can bear witness to a timeless God and be faithful to or betray an unchanging absolute Thou.

between an historical religion and the particular faith of those who believe in it, from "religion in general or faith in general" [II, 131]. The philosopher, he says, "who appreciates the exigency for transcendence in its fullness," which we know is for something which has eternal intrinsic value, namely, being or God, cannot be satisfied with anything in this finite temporal world. He or she may, therefore, be prompted by that exigency to "faith in general," that is, to believe in some unspecified kind of sacred, transcendent being or beings.[8] Obviously, he is talking about believers he earlier designated as naturally religious. Such believers "fall short of any conversion to any particular historical religion" and its faith in a specific notion of God. Conversion depends on grace which is a gift which cannot be produced or merited by human efforts and so, although at its limit, philosophy may perceive the possibility of conversion, it is powerless to bring it about. For conversion, Marcel explains, a person "will have to discern the action of the living God or again a recognizable call" [II, 133] which he or she must answer, a call (vocation) to become a witness to the living God in a particular historical religious community or church.

Of course, one is free to accept or reject that invitation. Even believers of long standing must realize that their conversion is not accomplished once and for all and that they must continue to freely choose to accept God's call; therefore, they should spiritually interact with recent converts to their community not condescendingly but with charity and respect, for they themselves are not much more than novices [II, 134]. Since conversion may involve accepting a particular church, a philosopher who is not a member may be better able to understand it, Marcel says, if he or she views the church not primarily as a social institution but as "a concrete intelligible milieu" [II, 135], which means, from his remarks last year, a community made up of persons joined in love who together seek and bear witness to the light of truth which is God. Outside the church as a milieu of "incarnate intersubjectivity" [II, 108], he cautions, "faith is in danger of being degraded into a rather erratic disposition or even to an unguided phenomenon" [II, 135] and that means, as we shall see later, the church's role in safeguarding genuine faith and distinguishing it from error is extremely important.

For now, Marcel repeats his insistence that the "starting point ... for the philosopher who wishes to direct his thought to faith ... is to take

8   Remember, philosophers are all who recognize their ontological exigency and seek answers to ultimate questions about reality.

the question of faith seriously or, if you like, to recognize its reality,"
even if "he cannot say that he personally adheres to this faith" *[II, 135]*.
That prompts the objection that to recognize or take faith seriously is to
"give faith the benefit of a favorable prejudice," but shouldn't we instead
maintain "a strictly neutral attitude towards it?" *[II, 136]*. His response
is typical. The one who raises such an objection thinks of faith in God
as posing a hypothesis about God's reality, a hypothesis "capable of being
either confirmed or disproved by experience;" however, faith in God, as
he has said so often, does not involve an hypothesis about the existence of
some empirical being. Furthermore, purification of faith means becoming
more open to being and more liable to being penetrated by its light but
that describes a relation of participation of the believer or witness in the
being/light to which he or she testifies *[II, 136]*. I might add that later
he offers the same reply to the objection that it is fallacious to argue from
the testimony of the believer to the existence of the being believed in. The
objection views the believing witness as external to the being believed in
when their true relation is one of participation *[II, 139]*.

If the purity of my faith is proportionate to my openness to participation in being or light, then it follows that "the more unconditional
my faith is in a transcendent Being, the more genuine [or pure] it will
be" *[II, 137]*. Of course, there will always be temptations to set conditions on God, for example, to believe only so long as no tragedy befalls
me, and the temptation will be greater, the more my "relation to God
has not been a living relation" of participation. However, secondary
reflection will "realize that a being in whom faith really resides, will
undoubtedly find ... by the help of God's own presence the strength
to repel this temptation" *[II, 138]*. Clearly that must be the case if we
believe, explicitly or implicitly, and participate in an absolute Thou who
is always united to us in love. That is also true if "the relation between
the living God and the faithful" is conceived, as Marcel suggests here,
"as *fatherhood in its purity*," where the father is the one portrayed in the
parable of the prodigal son *[II, 140]*.

Now it is all well and good for him to insist that the believer's relation
to God is not a relation to an external object whose existence can be
empirically verified. However, to maintain that the believer participates
in the God in whom he or she believes seems to beg the question of
God's reality, for participation in God presupposes the reality of that
God—one cannot participate in what is not. But then the question is,
on what basis does Marcel maintain that a believer in God is not just

deluded and engaging in wishful thinking but does truly participate in God?

As we know, he bases his conclusions on the analysis of experience, in this case "any experience we may have of authentic faith in such witnesses as it is our fortune to meet," especially those "in whom faith has withstood trials to which it would have seemed natural for it to succumb" [II, 138]. Does that mean we must simply accept as authentic the testimony of all purported believers that the God in whom they believe exists? That can hardly do since throughout history people have sincerely believed in all kinds of alleged divinities, including some who demanded the sacrifice of children, oppression of women and nonwhite races, and the slaughter of infidels. Even today we see many who are willing to give their lives and destroy others for such gods and, surely, Marcel would not accept their faith at face value and agree that it involves participation in an absolute Thou or loving Father. But, then, to rephrase our question, how can he (or we) distinguish between those believers whose faith is authentic and who, therefore, do truly participate in God and others whose faith is not authentic and who, therefore, do not participate in God—even though they may sincerely believe they do?

The issue I am pressing here is similar to the objection I posed in my commentary on Chapter 5 where I suggested that Marcel's argument, that Being or an absolute Thou must (at least implicitly) be experienced by those who pledge unconditional fidelity and love to a creature, proves too much. After all fanatics testify by their lives and self-sacrifice that they too are unconditionally faithful to and love some human beings (for example, Hitler, Jim Jones, Osama bin Laden) and some causes (the Third Reich, Greater Serbia, a rigid Islamic theocracy). Yet Marcel would hardly grant that such believers do in fact experience or participate in a being possessing eternal value or an absolute Thou. So again the question, does he have any way of deciding which people of faith do encounter and participate in God and which people of faith do not, even though they honestly believe they do? As far as I can see, he offers no answer to those questions in this chapter or anyplace in *The Mystery*..... Fortunately, one is suggested in *Tragic Wisdom and Beyond* and it involves joining together his notion of purity and his conception of a concrete intelligible milieu or community (or church) of believers who together bear witness to God.

In *Tragic Wisdom*... Marcel argues that only someone who is purified, that is, who adopts the proper perspective and ontological humility, only that person is able to experience Being or an absolute Thou or Holy God and so be in a position to assess the authenticity of the faith of other purported believers in God. Now if a purified believer joins in "fraternal comprehension" with other self-proclaimed believers, that is, lovingly unites with them in a "fraternal community,"[9] he or she will be able to some degree to comprehend the faith of those alleged theists as well as that to which or whom they witness. Fraternal "comprehension is at the heart of witness...[and] *permits the recognition of witness,*"[10] Marcel writes. In other words, if a purified believer joins in love with those who claim to be faithful witnesses to God, that individual will participate to some extent in those witnesses' faith experiences. And since the relation of believers to what they believe in is one of participation or union, to share in the believers' faith experiences will mean to participate to some degree in that to which they pledge themselves. Thus, by sharing in the experiences of those who claim to believe in God, a purified believer will be able to some extent to "comprehend" what they believe in and to "recognize" whether they actually are responding to something or someone of eternal intrinsic value (Being), an absolute Thou or a Holy God.

However, to speak of the comprehension and recognition of only a single purified believer is awfully limited. While it may be possible for one person of faith to lovingly comprehend and truly assess the faith of others, a much more reliable comprehension and recognition would be one undertaken by a whole community of believers. Recall in this connection Marcel's earlier remarks about the vital importance of the church in safeguarding genuine faith and distinguishing it from error. His point, I take it, is that a concrete intersubjective milieu or community of believers united in love and dedicated to the pursuit of the truth that is God, who join in loving unity with other alleged theists, are far more likely to accurately comprehend and recognize the character and object of the latter's faith than is a single individual. May I add that Marcel would have similar advice for believers who in their moments of doubt wonder whether they really do encounter God in their faith. Go to those witnesses who are more pure, more sensitive to, and filled with the Divine Presence, those who radiate the light of being most intensely. Invite them to lovingly participate in your faith experience for they have the eyes that

---

9   TW, 185.

10   TW, 182. My emphasis and translation of *Pour une sagesse tragique* (Paris: Librairie Plon, 1968), 266.

can see and the ears that can hear. They will be able to comprehend or discern the authenticity of your faith. Better yet, join with an incarnate community of such believers, a church, made up of countless people of faith now and throughout the centuries; they will be even more capable of distinguishing genuine from false faith and of guiding and strengthening you in keeping your faith authentic *[II, 135].*[11] In an interesting twist, he also suggests that by their encounters with believers, those who claim they do not believe may be stimulated to reflect on their experience and ask themselves whether in the final analysis they are so sure that they are unbelievers, especially if they recognize that they, like believers, are in some way also totally committed to something or someone of eternal value.[12] Of course, for them or for us to acknowledge the testimonies of believers "in the fulness of their significance," that is, to grant that some believers do truly participate in and witness to God, "is in some way to become witnesses ourselves" *[II, 139].*

To apply the foregoing analysis to fanatics, if believers purify themselves and lovingly bond with such individuals and participate in their experience, they (the believers) may be able to gain some comprehension of that to which the fanatics are faithful. They may well discover that the fanatics are actually committed to genuine imperishable values, such as freedom or justice or truth[13] but that they believe, wrongly, that certain individuals or groups are out to destroy those values and that defending them justifies the use of violence. Or the fanatic might for some reason think that those values are restricted to a particular group or cause; that is, though they do experience genuine values, they mistakenly limit their scope. As we have noted repeatedly, Marcel holds that true values are universal in that they extend to all human beings. Finally, if believers sympathetically participate in their experience, they may discover that the fanatics are not completely willing to adopt the proper perspective and be totally open to the experience of being, or, in Marcel's language, the fanatics may be unwilling to undergo purification.

In the final six pages of the chapter, Marcel discusses the metaphysical status of a trial, that is, of something "which I feel at first that I cannot live through" *[II, 142]* and of evil. He rejects the idea that they are

---

11 CF, 7-8.

12 BH, 208-09. See also CF, 181-82.

13 Recall that in his discussion of opinion in Chapter 5, Marcel stated that it may contain an experience of true values.

"spiritual tests" set by God for his creatures because he considers that incompatible with his conception of God as a loving father like the father of the prodigal son. He also repeats what he said earlier about the mystery of evil, namely that we are not able to understand the "intimate meaning" of events that happen to us, such as trials, simply because we cannot adopt a God's eye view of things. He does add, however, that as we approach death we become more capable "of seeing ourselves in a light which allows the hidden meaning of events to filter through" [II, 142]. (Some say, for example, that an experience that was so painful at the time can be seen years later to have been very beneficial.) Marcel even goes so far as to say that for the philosopher "everything is in some way a trial" and he specifically cites "the disconcerting multiplicity of the empiric data which he has to take into account" [II, 143] without over simplifying it. That multiplicity can be viewed as a "protean evil," he states, which takes all kinds of shapes and which some philosophers have tried to reduce to unity, for example, by maintaining that all evil is privation or a lack of being. He himself suggests that that explanation may not be the whole story for there may also be "positive evil which is bound up with some radical perversion of will" [II, 143]. In the final analysis, he doubts that much progress can be made in the understanding of evil without the assistance of grace.

Marcel concludes by saying that we are now faced for the first time with the so-called problem of evil. (Apparently he has forgotten that he addressed that "problem" earlier in this volume [II, 72-75]). Since in our day the existence of evil is a major stumbling block for religious faith, we must reach a clear position about it, he says. For now, he simply asserts that evil and death are connected and "can in a certain sense be regarded as synonymous," for even the most fulfilled human being in whom grace dwells has not thereby attained "any immunity to the principles of death in the working of our universe" [II, 144]. I presume those "principles of death" are things like suffering, illness, destruction, despair, moral evil, and sin. In any case, that provides his transition to the next chapter on death and hope.

Pages in other works of Marcel that treat material of this chapter:
CF, 6-10, 181-82.   TW, 182-86.
PE, Chapter 3.   BH, 95-100, 207-10.
Problematic Man, 54-60.

9
DEATH AND HOPE

On the first page of this chapter Marcel advises us that in thinking about death we must find our way between two errors. One is not taking death seriously enough, when in fact it is an "*apparent* final value, which gives to human life a quality of tragedy;" the other is to make "a dogmatic affirmation of the final character of death" *[II, 146]*. Both may lead to despair, he points out and, indeed, today there are many possible sources of despair. One is to regard human beings as interchangeable units or machines which are capable of a certain output, "this output being the only justification of their existence." From that perspective humans are no longer "*thought of as beings*," he says, that is, as possessing "inalienable characteristics of uniqueness and dignity...attributes of the human soul created in the image of God" *[II, 148]*. In an interesting aside he notes that, while some nineteenth century philosophers such as Nietzsche and Marx believed that life in this world would acquire more significance when the majority rejected the notion of an afterlife, in fact the opposite has happened, life today has increasingly been viewed as worthless and "devoid of any intrinsic justification" or meaning *[II, 148]*. That view has led to an almost universal "dehumanizing way of behaving ... in a world which is more and more enslaved to the demands of technology" *[II, 149]*, for example, the demand that persons be valued only for their output or their contributions to some economic or political organization. Such a world is "consigned to death," he claims, by which he means it is incapable of resisting the fascination death has "over the man who has come to look on it as the final word."

On the other hand, it is true, he admits, that some who emphatically deny personal immortality have bravely sacrificed themselves for the good of others or for their conception of an ideal society. In order to understand their actions we need, "through an act of sympathy," to try and understand the "internal aspect of sacrifice," namely, the thoughts, feelings, and choices of those who offer their lives for others. Such sympathetic understanding was called "fraternal comprehension" in the previous chapter and he recalls that it was also used to understand self-sacrifice in Volume I.[1] When we participate sympathetically in the experience of an individual willing to sacrifice himself, we will find, Marcel claims, that "he feels sure without knowing it," that is, without being able to clearly conceptualize or articulate it, "that there will not be an end of him, but rather that he will survive ... in the reality for which he has sacrificed himself" because he participates in that reality *[II, 150]*. That, of course, raises the issue of immortality again, and, he now declares, it is about it that "the decisive metaphysical choice must be made" *[II, 151]*.

If human beings live only to die, he argues, then Macbeth's famous words—"life is a tale told by an idiot full of sound and fury signifying nothing"—"would have to be taken as the literal truth" *[II, 151]*. In a world dominated by technique, a world where intersubjective relations of love seem to be disappearing, death would be viewed simply as the discarding of a worn out defective machine. (Of course, to the eyes of faith that would be sacrilegious.) However, to speak as he did above about immortality involving a "decisive choice" is bound to raise objections from those who claim that no choice is involved in this matter because we are dealing with a "question of fact." They maintain that under the influence of science and critical philosophy, the notion of a hereafter should be discarded as imaginary and out of date. Others might contend that religion should not be tied to an improbable belief like personal survival and, moreover, that preoccupation with one's immortality is self-centered, while religion should be only God centered *[II, 152-53]*.

In response to the first objection, Marcel denies that questions about immortality are about matters of fact, where fact means "empirical data" *[II, 153]*. Just as to talk about God's reality is to refer to a being beyond empirical world, so too life after death refers to something transcending our physical world. To be more concrete, he returns to his earlier discussion of love and quotes again from one of his plays, "to love a being is to say, 'thou, thou shall not die'" *[II, 153]*. Now on what could such a "prophetic assurance" be based? From the point of view of those who insist that everything must be empirically verified, an assertion of survival after death directly contradicts the data of experience for insofar as the loved one "participates in the nature of things," he or she "is subject to destruction" *[II, 153]*. However, the crucial question is, "can destruction overtake that by which this being is truly a being,"

1   I, 165-67.

for it is "this mysterious quality which is aimed at in my love" *[II, 154]*. The one I love is both an object, a *that*, a thing, and a *thou* and, insofar "as he is a *thou*," Marcel asserts, "he is freed from the nature of things, and nothing that I can say about things," namely, that they cease to exist, "can concern him, can concern the *thou*" *[II, 154]*.[2]

Actually, the indestructibility in question refers more to the bond between me and my beloved, he says, and can be expressed this way: "whatever change may intervene in which I see before me, you and I will persist as one; the event which has occurred [death] ... cannot nullify the promise of eternity which is enclosed in our love, in our mutual pledge" *[II, 154-55]*. Still, even if one agrees that beings who love each other are united in a common bond and that that bond has within it an urge or demand for eternity, for the lovers want their love to last forever, how can we say, "that this exigency is satisfied in some depth of reality which eludes our sight?" *[II, 155]*.[3] To answer that question, Marcel states, will require dealing with "the metaphysical status of hope," which he will do after he responds to the second objection given above, namely, that to be concerned about one's survival after death is ego-centric and true religion should be centered only on God.

Marcel counters that objection by arguing that we can not "radically separate faith in God conceived in His sanctity [the Holy God referred to earlier] from any affirmation which bears on the intersubjective unity which is formed by beings who love one another" *[II, 155]*. How can that Holy God ignore our love or treat it as insignificant and annihilate it, he asks? Is it conceivable that a Holy God (who is also an absolute Thou) who "offers himself to our love" and thereby makes it possible in the first place, would call us to total self-giving and then "range himself *against* this same love in order to deny it, to bring it to nothingness?" *[II, 156]*. His argument here is rather condensed, so let me unpack it. As we know, Marcel holds that in order to offer unconditional love, love that has no temporal limits, to another creature, I must, at least vaguely and prereflectively, experience both my beloved and myself to be participating in a being that possesses *eternal* value, a being that can assure me that my loved one will *always* be worthy of my love and that I can *always* be assisted to be faithful to my commitment. Such a being,

---

2   The word "*tu*" is not capitalized in French, ME, II, 155, as it is in the translation.

3   My translation from French, ME, II, 155-56.

he has argued, can only be an absolute Thou who in love is perpetually united to us. Now such a God, he reasons, whose loving presence in his creatures calls them to give themselves totally to each other and assists them in doing so, such a God can not deny or annihilate their love. Of course, if their love is not annihilated, the lovers must be immortal. Perhaps we could also say that insofar as lovers experience each other to have values that are not limited in time, and only that experience can explain their offering unconditional love to each other, the lovers experience themselves and their love to transcend time.[4]

Marcel turns then to a discussion of hope and begins by distinguishing it from desire and from fear. (The French word he uses, *espérance*, can be translated either as hope or trust.[5] I think the English term trust usually renders his meaning more accurately.) The opposite of trust he states, is not fear but "a state of depression... the state of a being who expects nothing from himself, nor from others, nor from life" [II, 158].[6] Hope or trust, on the other hand, is akin to courage, he explains, courage in the face of some kind of captivity, which may be something specific like an illness or something general such as the condition of every human being destined to die [II, 156-60]. Now trust is not just a desire or wish that there be some way out of that captivity; rather " to trust is to carry within me the personal assurance that however black things may seem, my present intolerable situation cannot be final; there has to be some way out" [II, 160]. Marcel's concrete illustration is of someone who hopes for the coming of a just world. That person does not just desire or prefer that such a world come to be; he "proclaims that this world *shall come* into existence" [II, 159]. Likewise, a sick person who trusts does not simply desire to be cured; "he tells himself 'you shall be cured'" [II, 161],— and that trust can actually promote his cure. To dismiss such a cure as only auto-suggestion fails to account for trust's real efficacy, he argues.

Besides, auto-suggestion is closed in on itself, while trust, he insists, is open—-but open to what? On what is the assurance present in trust based? Needless to say, if my hope is that a particular event occur, for example, that my disease be cured or that I be released from prison, I

---

4   Marcel points out that when he refers to love he does not mean only marital love but also friendship and filial relationships *[II, 157]*.

5   In this connection see BH, 74.

6   My translation from French, ME, II, 159.

may be disappointed. On the other hand, if my trust is open to some unseen world then it refers to "the sphere of the unverifiable" and so one could "see in it a mere mystification" because it looks like an evasion of reality [II, 162]. In response, Marcel asserts that "to hope is not essentially *to hope that*" some particular thing occur ("to desire," on the other hand, "is always to desire something") [II, 162]. In *Homo Viator*, where he treats it more extensively,[7] he writes that hope or trust should not be conditional for if it is, then if certain particular expectations of mine are not fulfilled, I despair. Instead, hope or trust should set no conditions or limits, then it can not be disappointed. Even if that is true, still, to repeat the above objection, isn't a hope which refuses to set conditions just an evasion of reality, an illusion indulged to avoid disappointment? As far as I can see, in the remaining pages of this chapter Marcel responds to that objection only obliquely at best.

In what looks at first like an aside, he suggests that hope may be another name "for the exigency for transcendence," the exigency for being which is "the driving force behind man the wayfarer" [II, 162]. By that he apparently means to emphasize that hope is not some trivial feature of our nature but is part of, or linked to, our deepest inner urge or exigency. As such, hope is indeed the "driving force" behind the goals we seek, the actions we perform, and the kind of persons we become.[8] But even if all that is true, how is it relevant to the above objection that alleged that hope is an evasion of reality?

As if to offer some response to that objection, Marcel insists, again, on "the sacred element ... [in] any and every human existence," which he now calls "a certain absolute" [II, 163].[9] That absolute must be recognized, he says, else we have no reason for rejecting euthanasia (and, I might add, slavery, genocide, infanticide and other horrendous evils). What follows next, however, is extremely obscure for he refers in very abstract terms to the "incomprehensible unity of aspects which at first we

7   HV, Chapter 2.

8   Marcel said much the same about faith. What I believe in will determine the goals I seek and create the kind of person I become. In HV he says hope and faith are inseparable, HV, 46.

9   That is his affirmative answer to a question he asked at the end of Volume I, 216-18, whether there is something of absolute value, something sacred, at stake in human life? To refer to life as absolute, rather than relative, means, I believe, that it possesses value universally, that is, at all times and places. It can never lose its inherent value.

thought should be dissociated" [II, 164] but does not say what "aspects" he has in mind. I can only propose that he is asserting, as he did earlier,[10] that while we may at first separate the fact of human life and any value attributed to it, they are united, that is, human life has *inherent* value and meaning— and it has that because it comes from God, and so can be considered sacred and absolute. My interpretation is supported by his statement which follows, namely, that the best way to interpret that unity of life and value is "as an expression of a divine gift" [II, 164]. As he explained in Chapter 7, we can be assured that human life has been endowed with intrinsic value and meaning only if God reveals himself to be its source, which is to say only if God reveals that life is his gift.[11] Of course, if human life is a sacred and absolute divine gift, it makes sense to say, as Marcel does, that there is "in its essence ... perhaps, a certain perennialness" and that life "holds within itself a promise of resurrection" [II, 164], for a sacred and absolute gift from God must survive death. If death were its final destiny, Hamlet's statement about life's meaninglessness would be correct. Marcel concludes the chapter by stating that "what matters today is that man should rediscover the sense of the eternal" [II, 165], the sense that we have an eternal dignity and destiny beyond the temporal world.

Let me try and put together these final reflections of Marcel on the connection of hope and our exigency for being, and on the sacred, absolute character of human life as a divine gift, and suggest how they can be brought to bear on the objections and questions raised earlier. One objection was that unconditional trust, a trust that can never be disappointed by anything that happens or does not happen in this world, is an evasion of reality concocted to avoid disappointment. By linking trust with our exigency for being and then asserting that human life is a sacred, absolute, divine gift, Marcel may be implying that trust is grounded in an experience of being (intrinsic eternal value) in human beings, and humans have intrinsic eternal value because they are gifts from God. And, indeed, he does assert elsewhere that hope or trust "is rooted in being"[12] which means that trust is not an evasion of reality,

---

10   II, 61-2.

11   II, 120-22.

12   CA, 187, my translation from French, *Positions et approaches concrètes du mystère ontologique*, 2nd ed. (Paris: Beatrice-Nauwelaerts, 1967), 75.

as the objection claimed, but a penetration into its very depths where it discovers the presence of being.

Earlier, Marcel also posed a related, more general, question. Since hope or trust is described as possessing the "assurance" that in the final analysis we will escape death, on what is that assurance based? As a first step in answering, let us become more clear about the nature of that assurance. In *Tragic Wisdom*... he identifies the "primordial existential assurance," which is the "fundamental experience" he calls "the *gaudium essendi*, the joy of existing," with hope or trust.[13] In other words, trust is the joyful assurance and fundamental experience that life is a gift. On what is that assurance based? Marcel's answer, as we just noted above, is that hope "is rooted in being," or, in more detail, "Hope consists in asserting that there is at the heart of being, beyond all data, beyond all inventories and all calculations, a mysterious principle in connivance with me, which cannot but will what I will, at least if what I will is really worth willing and is, in fact, willed with the whole of my being."[14] Of course, we know that mysterious "principle" at the heart of being is an absolute Thou and in the following lines from *Homo Viator* he says precisely that. "Absolute hope, inseparable from a faith that is likewise absolute ... appears as a response of the creature to the infinite Being to whom it is conscious of owing everything that it has.... From the moment that I abase myself in some sense before the absolute Thou who in his infinite condescension has brought me forth out of nothingness ... I forbid myself ever again to despair."[15] Despair would be an act of treason, he asserts, since it declares, in effect, that a loving God has abandoned me. Let me add that if a loving God will never abandon me, we have another reason for trusting that we will live after death. In parallel with his earlier argument about love and immortality, Marcel could reason that a loving, Holy God, an absolute Thou, who implanted in us a deep demand for being, that is, for something possessing *eternal intrinsic value*, something which is ultimately Himself, could not call us to lovingly participate in Himself and then deny us the fulfillment of our demand for eternal union with Him?[16]

---

13 TW, 42-43; HV, 43.

14 CA, 184. See also BH, 79.

15 HV, 46-47. See also, 152.

16 HV, 46-47, indirectly suggests such an argument.

To conclude, let me note that in his discussion of hope or trust, Marcel is not trying to prove that people do trust. As with fidelity and love, he considers it a matter of experience that there are people who trust, even in the face of great suffering and inevitable death, that ultimately life is a meaningful gift not terminated by death. His goal is to discover what makes such trust possible and his answer is that those who trust unconditionally must experience, at least dimly and implicitly, that life is a gift from an absolute Thou. Nothing less could explain and justify their hope. And again, Marcel does not think that only professed theists hope unconditionally. All who trust that in the final story, death cannot be the last word because life makes sense, reality is on our side, all will be well, must experience the revelation that an absolute Thou is the heart of being—whether they say so or not, whether they are reflectively aware of doing so or not. Either the person who hopes unconditionally experiences, at least dimly, a loving God or his or her trust is unintelligible, foolish, and self-deceptive for life is meaningless since in the final analysis death reigns As always, Marcel grants that we are free to choose either alternative but the second disregards our widespread experiences of the sacredness of human life and the richness of the universe, and dooms us to a despair which renders us powerless in the face of human depravity.[17]

Pages in other works of Marcel that treat material of this chapter:

HV, 143-54, Chapter 2.   CA, 183-88.
CF, 77-78, 140-44.   EBHD, 136-44.
BH, 74-79, 93-94.   MJ, 62-64, 220-22, 232-33.
TW, 42-45.

---

17 TW 42-44; CF, 141-43; HV, 63.

IO

CONCLUSION

His final chapter in the Gifford lecture series begins with Marcel stating that he wants to bring together "the principle themes" he has set forth in these lectures so that each reader "may become aware of the importance they hold for his own life" [II, 166]. This is especially pressing today since there exists a situation without precedence in human history, namely, the "extreme probability that we are heading for catastrophes," such as nuclear warfare, that might well render our entire planet almost uninhabitable [II, 167]. That probability is especially disturbing since that destruction would not be due to natural disasters like earthquakes or floods but would be the result of deliberate human acts, even though, he conjectures, it might also involve greater than human or "devilish" powers [II, 168]. Along with violence against human beings, the last few centuries have also seen a great deal of human violence against nature, such as the unbridled use and waste of natural resources. That is especially shameful, he remarks, since nature and its resources are gifts from our Creator and Father, "the unrepresentable and uncharacterizable Being who constitutes us as existents" [II, 170].

Given our present tragic situation, what sort of help can the type of philosophy he has sketched in these lectures offer us, Marcel asks [II, 167]? Even though he has succeeded "in defining at least with a minimum of precision the spiritual attitude which we must adopt" today, and he specifically mentions faith and hope, he wonders if his treatment of them might be "not only ineffective but also untimely" [II, 168]. Needless to say, he does not think that is the case and to highlight their relevance, he launches into a further discussion of faith and hope along with charity or love.[1] His first move is to stress the indissolubility of the three, meaning that a person can not possess one without the others. As we noted earlier, love includes faith in the immortality of the beloved and trust in an absolute Thou; also, people can be faithful to someone or some cause only if they love them; hope or trust involves

---

1   He points out that although he has not used the term charity until now, he has continually talked about intersubjectivity as a bond of love and so it is "nothing but charity itself" (II, 170).

belief in a loving Thou at the center of reality. Hope, he adds now, also involves love or charity because it is not self-centered but is "hope for us—for all of us," that is, for the community I make up with all those who share my journey *[II, 171]*. He has explained this earlier, he says, probably referring to his treatment of hope in *Homo Viator* where, as we saw in the previous chapter, it is described as unconditional trust in an absolute Thou.[2] Because an absolute Thou has created and loves *all* human beings, trust in him must recognize that he wills the salvation (to be defined later) of them all and that prompts Marcel, once again, to consider his notion of universality. The universal community, he says, is not merely an arithmetic collection or sum of indistinguishable units, for arithmetic operations can apply only to things or persons treated as things. The universal is rather a "supra-personal" or "polyphonic" unity of all human beings which respects and preserves the uniqueness and dignity of each of them. As he explained earlier when talking about values, to claim they are universal is to say they apply to all human beings, each of whom is a unique individual with inherent worth. Accordingly, the universality he is talking about here is, he states "a will for non-exclusion ... a kind of spiritual welcoming" of everyone *[II, 172]*. Since we have no way of knowing whether all humans do in fact attain salvation, for as creatures we are never "in the position of an absolute judge"[3] who could exclude or give preference to some over others, perhaps on the basis of their moral worth, we should, like our Creator, will the salvation of everyone.

That does not mean, however, that hope for the salvation of all is just a prudential attitude or standpoint we have to adopt because we do not know the fate of every one. That would be equivalent to saying "we have to act *as though* we were hoping for all of us," although in reality we are not. Instead of a prudential attitude, genuine trust that all will be saved is rooted, as we have seen, in the assurance of an absolute Thou at the heart of reality, and that, he states, is where faith comes in for it "gives to hope its intelligible framework" *[II, 173]*. I interpret him to mean that the trust that all will be saved involves belief in the reality of an absolute Thou and that belief makes the trust understandable. To say that faith provides intelligibility to hope also means that faith should

---

2   HV, 46-47, 60-61, 152.

3   The term *absolut* in the French, ME, II, 173, is omitted in the translation.

not be interpreted "in a purely voluntarist sense," namely, as a pure act of will,[4] for it is not just a blind choice or a leap in the dark which lacks all cognitive or experiential basis. Rather, its basis, he claims, is that "each of us is in a position to recognize that his own essence is a *gift* ... that he himself is a gift and that he has no existence at all through himself" [II, 173]. In other words, we can recognize that we are unable to confer on ourselves our being as well as our intrinsic worth and yet, we can also recognize or experience that our lives are not just accidental results of blind chance but have value and meaning conferred on them. And that means they are gifts and our awareness of that, however murky, entails an at least implicit awareness that a loving Creator or absolute Thou is their source. It is that awareness of an absolute Thou that faith responds to and which makes trust intelligible. Of course, as he has said so often, since the experience that life is a meaningful gift is not one of overwhelming clarity or certitude, we retain the freedom, the "decisive option," to accept the less than conclusive experience and believe in a loving Thou as life's source, or to reject that experience and deny the existence of an absolute Thou. That denial will mean that in the final analysis we will have to center ourselves solely on ourselves—a choice Marcel labels "demonic" [II, 194].

Yet if faith rests on such cloudy experiences, couldn't someone argue that the basic question remains unanswered, namely, does God exist or not, and that to answer it affirmatively we need to prove rationally that God is. We seem to have two alternatives. Either we reduce faith to the purely subjective experience of the believer and then it becomes an "incommunicable psychic event" which has no universal significance, or we must attempt to devise a logical demonstration of the existence of God, one that in principle all people, at least all of good faith, could accept [II, 173-74]. Marcel rejects both of those alternatives and proceeds to "an analysis of the phenomenological conditions of the act of proving." His analysis here in *The Mystery...* is a shortened version of an earlier one in *Creative Fidelity.*[5] Proof, he states in that earlier work, involves a claim made to another (or myself as other) that there is a necessary connection ("essential unity" [II, 174]) between something accepted by both of us as true (for example, that the world exists) and some other

---

4   Marcel believes that the Danish philosopher and theologian Soren Kierkegaard (1813-1855) held a voluntarist position about faith, II, 177.

5   CF, 176-77.

truth (for example, that God exists).[6] The claim that the first truth must be connected to the second is not made because the prover possesses some special power but because he or she has "a certain degree of inner concentration" of thought which enables him or her to see the logical steps that unite the two truths. In other words, the bond the prover sees between them is not just "a subjective datum," that is, it is not a purely internal and private phenomena within the prover, but is a real linkage between two truths and so in principle can also be recognized by others who also have a certain degree of inner concentration of thought [II, 174].

The fact is, Marcel notes, that historical proofs that have been offered for the existence of God have not been convincing even to some of those who have expounded them in great detail and that can hardly be because such people have not understood them. Still, we should not dismiss the proofs as totally sophistic either for, after all, "certain distinguished minds found them adequate."[7] Therefore, those who do not accept the proofs should not claim they are intellectually superior to those who are satisfied by them and the latter should not judge the former to be guilty of ill will [II, 175]. In fact, if we intelligently sympathize with those who do not accept the proofs, we may find, he suggests, that they reject them, not because of ill will, but because they consider an affirmation of God incompatible with some fundamental data of experience, such as the existence of evil (for example, the suffering of innocent children) or of human freedom (a Creator would significantly limit human freedom). If that is the case, then those who accept and those who reject the proofs lack even a minimal agreement on ends and values, Marcel points out, for they do not even agree on whether God's existence or proof of it would be a good or bad thing. The history of modern philosophy, he adds, offers many examples of atheism (not believing in God) being replaced by anti-theism, namely, "the will that God should not be" [II. 176].

Of course, it is precisely the atheist that the proofs of God's existence are designed to persuade. The paradox is that they are mostly ineffectual when it comes to convincing an unbeliever and, conversely, when belief

---

6   Reasoning from the world's existence to God's has traditionally been called the "cosmological proof" [II, 174].

7   CF, 178.

is present, and most who accept them are believers,[8] "they seem to serve no useful purpose." Indeed, "if a man has experienced the presence of God ... he has no need of proofs" and may even consider the very idea of a demonstration as disparaging his experience of the sacred *[II, 176]*. Of the two alternatives, proof or faith, Marcel repeats what he has said so often, it is the faith experience, the testimony, of the believer, not logical arguments, that "is the central and irreducible datum" for his kind of philosophy *[II, 176]*. (He adds, somewhat parenthetically, that when God's presence in human experience is no longer recognized or acknowledged and "man models himself on Lucifer" by embracing anti-theism, he can be awakened to God's presence only if, prompted by grace, he undergoes conversion. Of course, conversion is outside the realm of philosophy.)

Speaking of God's presence, Marcel states that paradoxically it provokes distress and anguish on the one hand and love and joy on the other. Although he does not explain his statement, I imagine that distress and anguish occur because to experience God is at the same time to experience our insignificance, powerlessness, and total dependence on an all powerful being completely beyond our control. On the other hand, since God's presence is the presence of an absolute Thou who loves us and promises fulfillment of our ontological exigency, it should provoke love and joy. To see more clearly that "the last word must be with love and joy," he says "we must emphasize the intelligible aspect of faith" for faith is bound together with "the spirit of truth," a spirit that is "a light which is seeking for the light" *[II, 177]*.

Once again he does not explain what he means but I suggest that he is making the same point that he did earlier in this chapter, namely, faith is not a blind leap in the dark nor a pure act of will as "the voluntarist error" considers it. The *"I believe"* of an individual is a "concrete unity" of intelligence and will *[II, 178]*, he stresses, for faith entails both a free choice and some intelligibility and truth, that is, some light. As we have seen so often, faith for Marcel contains an experience, albeit vague and unclear, of the presence of the Holy God or absolute Thou. To say it is joined to "the spirit of truth" means that faith loves, and hence seeks, even more light, a fuller experience of God, the uncreated Light. And, "the more I tend to raise myself towards this Uncreated Light," that is, the more I purify myself and humbly open myself to God's presence, "the more I in some way advance in faith." Marcel describes the coming

8   CF, 179.

together of faith and light, that is, faith's experience of God or Uncreated Light, as "nuptial joy" [II, 178], a joy in the light I love and already possess to some degree, even as I seek to possess it more. Because through faith I already possess some of the light (or truth) I love and seek, and since the Light I possess and seek is an absolute Thou who promises fulfillment of my love, the last word is, as he says, "with love and joy."

Although the concrete act of faith is a unity of intellect and will, intelligibility and free choice, there is, Marcel acknowledges, "bound to be a fringe of hesitation and even of unspoken refusal" around it [II, 178], for, except for the saint, none of us *fully* believe in or commit ourselves to God. That raises the question, to what extent does our belief or lack of it "depend on us"?[9] To what extent is faith our free act if it involves God's revelation and grace? In response Marcel suggests that while only God can grant us grace, we have a responsibility "to rid ourselves of prejudices which block the path to faith or, again, to make ourselves disposable to grace" [II, 178].[10] In his earlier terminology, we must purify ourselves. Yet even to do that, he concedes, "implies in its origin something which is of the same order as grace" [II, 179], which I understand means some kind of Divine assistance. Of course, since everything involves divine assistance, for it is all God's gift, the saint may sincerely proclaim that not just faith but absolutely "everything is grace" [II, 179]. However, were I to say those words, my utterance would not be totally sincere, Marcel says, since I do not totally believe it; my faith is always mixed with hesitation and refusal, as he said above. While I may affirm that the saint is correct "without that faith becoming absolutely my own," if I try to remain in such an ambivalent position without entering onto the saint's road to sanctity, there is a danger that my position will turn into a lie. For if I do not follow the saint, it may well be that in spite of what I say, I do not really believe that his or her words are true. On the other hand, if I try to follow the saint, even if I am not completely successful, "it can help me on the road to salvation" [II, 180].

His use, again, of the word salvation prompts Marcel to investigate the purely philosophical meaning of that term and he devotes most of the remainder of the chapter to that task. Not surprisingly, we shall see that many, if not all, the features he attributes to salvation are also

9   My translation from French, ME, II, 179.
10   I have slightly modified the translation from ME, II, 179.

ingredients of what in Chapter 3 he called being as fullness or *being par excellence*, that which would totally fulfill our exigency for being. For example, he asserts that, "salvation is nothing if it does not deliver us from death," just as earlier he suggested that, since it fulfills our exigency for eternal being, *being par excellence* must be eternal. It is fantasy, he insists here, to think that deliverance from death can occur in our temporal, physical world "whose very structure makes it liable to death" *[II, 180]* and no advances in technology can change the fact that we are mortal. (He also suggests that death may be the price we pay for sin but does not pursue the point.)

The mention of sin leads Marcel to digress briefly and discuss that topic, even though, he admits, we cannot comprehend it, presumably because it is fundamentally a theological notion. In the first place, by sin he does not necessarily mean individual sin for no matter how virtuous we may be "each one of us is involved," he argues, "in countless structures in which a spirit of good faith cannot fail to perceive the presence of sin" *[II, 181]*. (My illustration: each of us, as participants in and supporters of the politics and economy of our country, contributes in some way, whether we want to or not, to national and international structures that result in enormous imbalances in the distribution of the world's resources and wealth and, therefore, terrible poverty for millions.) As for the definition of sin, Marcel proposes the following: "all authentic sin is sin against the light, in other words, against the universal." As we know, by the universal he means all human beings; therefore, sin against the universal means ignoring, rejecting, or failing to love some human beings and at its root, he says, "it is the act of shutting oneself in on oneself or of taking one's own self as center" *[II, 181]*. Again, this is not just a matter of individual acts, for sin, or, more accurately, sinners have made a world or "anti-kingdom" whose structures are infected with indifference, hatred and oppression of others, a world where death may not be literally the "wages of sin," but surely "a world in which death is in some way *at home*" *[II, 181]*. To conquer that world by advancing the universal will be very difficult he admits for we will have to become engaged in "conditions which are not of our choosing," and, I would add, are deeply ingrained in our society, such as its unjust social and economic structures which make up the concrete situation in which we must follow our vocation to build a universal human community *[II, 182]*.

After another briefer digression into the philosopher's need for imagery, else he or she deals only with abstractions, Marcel returns to his main topic, salvation. Salvation is "better conceived by us as a road rather than a state," he asserts, and so while it may be "indistinguishable from peace," it would not be a static peace but a living one, "a progress in love and truth, that is, a consolidation of an intelligible city ... a city of souls" [II, 183]. That city sounds exactly like the community of those animated by the love of truth and of other human values, who delight in participating with each other in building that community.[11] That is to say, that city is another name for being as fullness. Of course, since he believes that salvation delivers us from death, that living community or city of love and truth can be in its absolute fullness only on the other side of death, perhaps that is why he also calls it a city of *souls*. In other works he refers to it as "the *Pleroma* which is Being,"[12] a promised world containing "universal communion" and "fullness of life,"[13] and a "real and *pleromatic* unity where we will be all in all."[14] Needless to say, it is what in Chapter 3 of this volume he called *being par excellence* [II, 51].

To speak of salvation as involving progress in love and truth does not mean, however, that human history itself is necessarily progressing in that direction. In fact, Marcel states, there is no way philosophically to know if history is progressing to or regressing from that ideal. The eighteenth century view that human history is advancing toward some sort of fulfillment becomes "a completely arbitrary postulate" [II, 183] once it is divorced from the Christian world view which it unknowingly drew upon. Surely, the terrible atrocities of the twentieth (and early twenty-first) centuries make that postulate doubtful in the extreme. But the primary reason we cannot predict the direction of history, he declares, is that progress toward a community of peace, love, and truth requires an awakening of human consciousness that can come about only by a conversion whose conditions, as he has so often said, "lie beyond the power of our own incentive." In fact, they "are almost certainly of the miraculous order" [II, 184], by which he means no doubt the order of Divine grace. It is, however, within our powers, he says, to see that conversion can not just affect the will, by assisting it to

---

11   See my commentary on II, Chapter 3, 155-58.

12   EBHD, 141.

13   TW, 142. See also EBHD, 89, 91-92.

14   EBHD, 141.

change from willing sin to willing virtue, it must also affect the intellect for conversion is also a change "in the light thrown upon life," that is, on the truths and values human beings perceive. That change in light, he suggests, will involve a "supra-temporalization" of life *[II, 185]*.

Supra-temporalization of life apparently consists of viewing it from the perspective of eternity. (Recall that at the end of the previous chapter he said that "what matters today is that man should rediscover the sense of the eternal" *[II, 165]*.) That perspective means that, "We must maintain that in so far as we are not things ... we belong to an entirely different world-dimension and it is this dimension which can and must be called supra-temporal" *[II, 186]*.[15] Marcel has talked about that dimension of ourselves many times in these lectures. In Volume I he discussed the deep dimension of our selves which is supra-temporal or eternal, namely, our essential spiritual self which endures throughout our changing temporal history. In this second volume that supra-temporal dimension has been called our being, that part of us which is experienced, especially in love and fidelity, as possessing eternal value and dignity and, therefore, not ending at death. Our being or eternal dimension is what invites unconditional commitments of love and fidelity and it is that part of ourselves which we pledge when we unconditionally commit ourselves to someone or some cause. Marcel has also stressed that our supratemporal or eternal dimension is not insulated or isolated from others. From our beginnings and throughout our lives we are joined with others in all kinds of intersubjective relationships, of which the most loving will continue after death, for our salvation is an eternal and universal city or community of souls united in love and truth.

As he concludes his lectures, he insists that the dead "whom we have never ceased to love" are part of that city even now for they make up a "living reality...which quite certainly surrounds us on all sides" and to which we belong *[II, 186]*. And philosophy should help "increase our awareness, even this side of death, of this reality" whose presence can just be "felt and even touched,"[16] for, he claims, we receive subtle but innumerable "solicitations" from and "infiltrations" of this "invisible

---

15 Marcel's use of the term "dimension" is significant for in an earlier lecture he had suggested that the dimension of eternity "beyond" the temporal world is not "*literally* supraterrestrial but dimensions or perspectives within a universe of which we apprehend only the one aspect which is in tune with our own organic-psychic structure" *[II, 157-58]*.

16 My translation from French, ME, II, 187.

world" [II, 187]. As always, we are free to ignore or minimize or otherwise withhold ourselves from that world since its invitations are so faint. Yet to the degree we respond to them, Marcel states, our earthly life acquires a dignity which it does not have if it is looked at as a brief aberration in the history of the material universe [II, 187].

Among the "solicitations" and "infiltrations" from the invisible world that he has in mind are, I believe, the kind of experiences he discusses in his early journal *Presence and Immortality*. One is the feeling some have that their dead loved ones are present to them and continue to have influence on their lives, that they "continue to make me what I am."[17] Some, for example, are consoled by talking to their dead spouses, some find their dead ancestors to be sources of inspiration and guidance, for others they evoke shame or regret. He highlights one such experience, the feeling some people have (even those not professedly religious) that they must be faithful to, as they might put it, the "memory" of a deceased loved one. Now does it make sense, he asks, to experience an obligation to be faithful to someone who was alive but is now totally extinct and exists only as an image in memory? If the deceased person no longer exists, why be faithful to a memory image of him or her which is an extremely poor substitute and will itself eventually deteriorate and vanish? If I respond that I am faithful to my father's memory out of love for *him*, aren't I admitting, Marcel argues, that "my love is for the being himself" not for a memory image of him?[18] In other words, isn't the "simplest and most economical hypothesis" to explain the widespread phenomena of fidelity to the dead, that the deceased person, and not just his or her image, is in some faint mysterious way still present to the living?[19] Similarly, considering the amount of impact they still have on me, isn't it more reasonable to believe it is my dead loved ones themselves who console, inspire, and challenge me and, thereby, "continue to make me what I am," not just a faint image of them in my memory? In speaking of the infiltrations of the dead, I should also mention Marcel's

17   PI, 122. Marcel refers to this phenomena in a number of places: PI, 78-80, 89, 177, 192, 238, 242-43; *Awakenings*, 165; CA, 189-92; *Searchings*, 70.

18   PI, 191. There are numerous places in PI where Marcel insists that it is not the image of a deceased loved one that I experience but the presence of the person. See, 73-82, 87-90, 144-45, 189-93. See also, CF, 189-92; BH, 97.

19   PI, 242.

lifelong conviction, based on metapsychical experiments with an ouija board that he participated in during World War 1, that some parapsychological phenomena do involve contact with the dead, granted that it is extremely rare and almost always terribly ambiguous.[20] Finally, I would add to the above infiltrations of the invisible world, the experiences Marcel has discussed throughout Volume II, experiences of love, fidelity, hope, and of life as a gift, every one of which he has argued contain, at least implicitly and inchoately, encounters with an absolute Thou or Holy God. They are all experiences of our participation, even now, in a supratemporal dimension of reality beyond this world and involve what in Volume I he called "glimpses" of an eternal realm, a realm that can be "felt and even touched" in this life.[21]

And he is convinced that we can become even more aware of that realm. Invoking a musical metaphor, Marcel claims that as we open ourselves more to the infiltrations of the invisible, we cease to be solitary soloists and gradually become conscious members of an orchestra which includes the dead, and also includes God. In Chapter 3 we wondered how God is present in the universal community of love and truth, the intelligible city of souls that is being *par excellence*; now we have our answer. God is not so much the conductor of that symphony, he says, rather, "He is the symphony in its profound and intelligible unity," in which we can hope to be included little by little by following our individual vocations [II, 187] But what does it mean to say that God is that symphony's, that universal community's, "profound and intelligible unity?" Since he does not explain what he means, let me offer the following suggestion. A bit earlier in this chapter, when he first mentioned the intelligible city of souls, Marcel suggested it was like "the Christian idea of the mystical body' [II, 183]; even earlier he made reference to "the indwelling of Christ" in the believer [II, 139]. By combining those theological notions we can shed some light on his conception of God as the unity of an eternal intelligible city. The mystical body of Christ refers to the mysterious spiritual union of the faithful in the risen Christ due to his dwelling in

---

20   He refers to those early experiments many times and to his life long conviction about "the reality of metapsychical phenomena," in "An Essay..." PE, 122. Also see, 123-24; CF, 31-32; *Awakenings* 96-106; PI, 241-43.

21   Note that this provides an affirmative answer to the questions he asked at the end of Volume I, 218-19, and which I posed at the end of my commentary on Chapter 3 of this volume: Can we in this life obtain some experience of our promised fulfillment in an eternal realm of *being par excellence?*

them and animating them with his life. Similarly, I suggest that Marcel considers God to be within all people living and dead giving them life and uniting them into a universal spiritual community (or symphony). The absolute Thou who is always deeply within each of us in love is, as he puts it in *Homo Viator*, the 'very cement" of our union.[22]

Marcel concludes this lecture and this series by asserting that everything he has said here "does not reach as far as revelation, properly so called, and dogma" [II, 187-88]. As we know, revelation "properly so called" refers to God's special communication of himself in particular historical religions or churches, in their sacred writings, creeds, doctrines, and so forth. The truths of such revelation (he specifically mentions the Christian dogmas of the Incarnation and the Redemption) cannot be arrived at by human efforts: "no effort of reason alone reflecting on experience can enable us to attain to these" mysteries.[23] Philosophy, however, does not depend on a special revelation but on revelation in a general sense. The faint experiences of the dead, of the hidden absolute Thou in love, fidelity and hope, of the Holy God in humility and prayer and in the feeling that life is a sacred gift, all are within the scope of philosophical reflection. That is because our human powers of analysis can detect the presence of God and of the dead, he states, in "mysteries enveloped in human experience as such."[24] To be sure, all revelations of God's presence are his generous gifts for they cannot be produced by our effort nor are they due to our merit. Nevertheless, human beings by their own powers are able to become aware of the "general revelations" of God present in experiences of fidelity, love, trust, prayer, and so forth. In fact, as we have repeatedly emphasized, Marcel holds that even someone who is "unfamiliar with any form of positive religion" can, at least nonreflectively, encounter the divine in those experiences. Yet, as we have also stressed, he never claims that his phenomenological analyses of various experiences conclusively demonstrate God's existence or human immortality; the experiential evidence is not that clear or overwhelming— which leaves us free to accept or reject it. However, if we continue to purify ourselves and remain open to the radiations and reflections of "that eternal Light...[which] has continually shone on us all

---

22   HV, 60.

23   CA, 196.

24   CA, 196. See also, PI 243-44; TW, 161, 182-86; MB, II, 122, 132-33.

the time we have been in the world," *[II, 188]* it will guide us, he firmly believes, on our "pilgrim road" to full participation in that symphony where that eternal Light is the intelligible bond and common life uniting all participants; where God, in other words, is "Love and Truth."[25]

Pages in other works of Marcel that treat material of this chapter:
TW, Chapter 4, 142-46, Chapter 12, 237-43, 251-56.
HV, 60-61, 151-53.　　　　　EBHD, Chapter 5.
CF, 79-80, 168, Chapter 9.　　PE, 122-24.
CA, 189-91, 194-96.　　　　　*Searchings,* 69-71.
BH, 97-98, 121.
PI, 73-82, 87-90, 122, 144-45, 189-93, 238, 241-44.

25　In MAMS Marcel writes that the word light "denotes what we can only define as the identity at their upper limit of Love and Truth," 262.

COMMENTATOR'S SUMMARY OF VOLUME II

Since Marcel devotes most of his second series of lectures to understanding being, my summary will do the same. One kind of being that he discusses briefly is what in later works he calls being as foundation. That being is a verb, the fact or act of being, the "is" of whatever is. It is not just one property among others but a transcendental since all entities and every part and feature of every entity must exercise the act of being and participate in it in order to *be*.

A second notion of being, which he describes more extensively, is being as fullness. It is the being that is the goal of our exigency or demand for being, which is also the exigency for God and the exigency for transcendence discussed in Volume I. Since it is the goal of our most basic and urgent exigency, being as fullness is the fundamental value we seek, a value that is sorely lacking in our overfunctionalized world. Marcel designates it as fullness in contrast to the emptiness or lack of value in a world which denies the inherent worth of every unique individual and the significance of intersubjective relations. Being as fullness, then, is a living intersubjective union of persons who acknowledge the intrinsic dignity of each human being. It is an intelligible community of persons animated by love for each other and for truth, who delight in seeking truth together. To some degree it can be experienced in this life, wherever there are loving communities of truth seekers, but only after death can it be present in its plenitude. In its plenitude it is an eternal universal community of the living and the dead joined in love and truth with God as their common life and bond of love, and Marcel calls it *being par excellence* and salvation.

His third referent for the meaning of being occurs when he speaks of a human person as a being rather than a thing or existent.[1] To attribute being to an individual is to assert that he or she possesses inherent value which will not cease at death. It is only because we experience in some way being, eternal value, in other people or causes that we commit ourselves unconditionally to them. Ultimately, Marcel maintains, unconditional commitments to creatures must be grounded in an

---

1   Marcel spends some time discussing the relation between being in this third sense and existence and is forced to broaden the meaning of the latter term beyond the sensuous presence of something.

encounter, faint and elusive though it may be, with an absolute Thou for only our participation in Him can provide us the assurance that we will receive the strength to be true to our pledges and that the beloved person or cause will always possess eternal value. Hope (or trust) also rests on an experience of being and of an absolute Thou for it involves the assurance that life is inherently meaningful because it is a sacred gift rather than the result of blind chance. That assurance is rooted in an at least prereflective experience, such as ontological humility and prayer, of an absolute Thou or Holy God, a transcendent being from whom we receive all that we are. An experience of that loving God at the heart of the universe brings us assurance that, no matter how bleak life becomes, our exigency for eternal salvation, being *par excellence*, will be satisfied.

In these pages Marcel also makes a very important distinction between two types of faith, of revelation, and of religion. One refers to faith in God or revelation in general which can be present in someone who is not a participant in any particular religious tradition but is, in his terminology, "naturally religious." The other, faith or revelation strictly speaking, contains specific beliefs in the God and revelation present in particular historical religions, churches, creeds, sacred texts, doctrines and so forth. That kind of faith is not attainable by human power but requires a personal conversion dependent on God's grace. The former, religious faith and revelation in general, is within the scope of philosophy for it involves natural religious experience that any human beings may have, whether or not they are professed believers in God or members of any particular religion. (Marcel is well aware that it is not just members of religious organizations or avowed theists who commit themselves unconditionally to others or feel assured that life is meaningful or are conscious of their utter dependence on some transcendent reality.) The naturally religious person's experiences of the Divine may be entirely nonreflective but they can be reflected on and analyzed philosophically by our ordinary human powers—as he himself has done in his examinations of humility, fidelity, love, and hope.

All the experiences of being or God that we have mentioned are not of some object within the empirical world and, therefore, are beyond scientific verification, yet, Marcel insists, they are not purely private subjective phenomena either. They are genuine experiences of reality, experiences that can be present in any human beings provided they purify themselves—which especially means free themselves from self-centeredness and humbly open themselves to others and to transcendence. Purification also involves a sympathetic loving union or participation with other subjects and so purified individuals can to some degree share the religious experiences of others and judge their authenticity. However, a loving community (or church) of purified believers is better able to comprehend and judge the validity of the faith of alleged believers and by participating in that community one's own faith can be strengthened and remain pure and genuine.

Finally, none of the experiences of being or God that Marcel has discussed are accompanied by overwhelming clarity or certitude. By his own admission, they are faint and elusive for most people and that leaves us the basic freedom to accept them and what they imply or disregard or dismiss them. But if we choose to reject our religious experiences, he believes that we are doomed to despair because our fundamental exigency for being will remain unfulfilled and our lives, extinguished by death, will in the final analysis be viewed as meaningless tales told by an idiot signifying nothing.

BIBLIOGRAPHY

This bibliography contains the works of Marcel I have referred to in this book. A complete bibliography of all of Marcel's works is available in K.R. Hanley's *Gabriel Marcel's Perspectives On The Broken World* cited below.

"An Essay in Autobiography" trans. M. Harari in *The Philosophy of Existentialism*. New York: Citadel, 1962. Originally published as "Regard en arrière" in *Existentialism Chrétien*, ed. E. Gilson (Paris: Plon. 1947).

Awakenings. trans. P. Rogers. Milwaukee: Marquette University Press, 2002. Originally published as *En chemin, vers quel éveil?* (Paris: Gallimard, 1971).

Being and Having. trans. K. Farrer. New York: Harper & Row, 1965. Originally published as *Être et Avoir* (Paris: Aubier, 1935).

"Concrete Approaches to Investigating The Ontological Mystery." trans K.R. Hanley in *Gabriel Marcel's Perspectives On The Broken World*. Milwaukee: Marquette University Press, 1998. Originally published as "Positions et approches concrète du mystère ontologique" (Paris: Desclée de Brouwer, 1933).

Creative Fidelity. trans. R. Rosthal. New York: Fordham University Press, 2002. Originally published as *Du refus a l'invocation* (Paris: Gallimard, 1940). It is now published in French as *Essai de philosophie concrète* (Paris: Gallimard, 1966).

The Existential Background of Human Dignity. Cambridge: Harvard University Press, 1963.

Homo Viator. trans. E. Crauford. New York: Harper & Row, 1962. Originally published as *Homo Viator* (Paris: Aubier, 1945).

Man Against Mass Society. trans. G.S. Fraser. Chicago: Regnery, 1962. Originally published as *Les hommes contre l'humain*. (Paris: La Colombe, 1951).

The Mystery of Being. Volume I trans. by G.S. Fraser; Volume II trans. by R Hague. South Bend, IN: St. Augustine's Press, 2001. Originally published as *Le Mystère de l'être* (Paris: Aubier, 1951).

Metaphysical Journal. trans. B. Wall. Chicago: Gateway, 1952. Originally published as *Journal métaphysique* (Paris: Gallimard, 1927).

Problematic Man. trans. B. Thompson. New York: Herder & Herder, 1967. Originally published as *L'Homme problématique* (Paris: Aubier, 1955).

Presence and Immortality. trans. M. Machado. Pittsburgh: Duquesne University Press, 1967. Originally published as *Présence et immortalité* (Paris: Flammarion, 1959).
Searchings. trans. W. Ruf. New York: Newman Press, 1967. Originally published as *Auf der Suche nach Wahrheit und Gerechtigkeit* (Freiburg im Breisgau: Verlag Knecht, 1964).

"Theism and Personal Relationships," *Cross Currents* I, (1950-51).

Tragic Wisdom and Beyond. trans. S. Jolin and P. McCormick. Evanston: Northwestern University Press, 1973. Originally published as *Pour une sagesse tragique et son au-dela* (Paris: Plon, 1969).

INDEX